MAKING THE MOST OF
THE LECTIONARY

MAKING THE MOST OF THE LECTIONARY

A user's guide

THOMAS O'LOUGHLIN

First published in Great Britain in 2012

Society for Promoting Christian Knowledge
36 Causton Street
London SW1P 4ST
www.spckpublishing.co.uk

British Library Cataloguing-in-Publication Data
A catalogue record for this book is available from the British Library

ISBN 978–0–281–06587–5
eBook ISBN 978–0–281–06588–2

Typeset by Graphicraft Ltd, Hong Kong
First printed in Great Britain by MPG Books
Subsequently digitally printed in Great Britain

Produced on paper from sustainable forests

For Kevin Lyon
who introduced the Lectionary to me

Contents

Contents

Preface

The Lectionary is the great undiscovered masterpiece of modern Christian liturgy: I have been engaged with it, in one way or another, since its first appearance, and with every passing cycle of readings I become more convinced of its value. I have now been training people in using the Lectionary for more than twenty years, and over that time have written commentaries on all its readings for Sundays and feasts, but its plan and organization still seem to induce more mystification than admiration. Indeed, at almost every in-service training day that is run for clergy, and at every such event run for 'ordinary' Christians, when one puts up an overhead (or now uses a PowerPoint slide) of its most basic structure there are gasps of surprise, such as: 'So that's why there has been so much of Matthew recently!' We have the Lectionary – some of us have had it for over 40 years now – but it has become habitual and customary without being absorbed. And while ministers have often become familiar with its cycles and its surface arrangement, they are often almost oblivious to the more subtle aspects of its planning and its larger christological orientation. Confronting this familiarity is the challenge of the Lectionary.

This book began life as lectures in church halls on cold evenings (sometimes one was glad that they even had a blackboard) and its contents developed in the slightly more comfortable surroundings of the conference rooms where clergy training days are held – to all who listened to me on those occasions, and especially who engaged me with their questions, I owe a debt of gratitude. I may never have learnt your name, but you may find your question or comment somewhere in these pages: thank you.

I also own a debt of gratitude to present and former colleagues who have encouraged me to set about this book: to Dr Juliette Day, now of the University of Helsinki, who pressed me repeatedly 'to teach the Lectionary'; to Dr Francisca Rumsey osc of Arkley who did likewise, and who generously read and commented on the typescript; to Revd Drs Alison Milbank and Simon Oliver (both in Nottingham) and Éoin de Bhaldraithe ocso (in Moone) who reminded me that this was a book that was worth writing; and, lastly, to Philip Law of

SPCK who was enthusiastic about the project from the moment I mentioned it to him. While I have benefited from much help and encouragement from all of them, for what appears, and for all its faults, I alone am responsible.

Thomas O'Loughlin
Nottingham

Abbreviations

AC	After Christmas
AE	After Epiphany
AP	After Pentecost
ASB	*The Alternative Service Book* (1980)
AT	After Trinity
BA	Before Advent
BCP	The Book of Common Prayer
BL	Before Lent
CWL	*The Common Worship Lectionary*
MR	*Missale Romanum* (1570)
P	Proper
PE	Post Easter
RCL	*Revised Common Lectionary*
RL	*Roman Lectionary* (1969)
RM	*The Roman Missal* (1969)
SC	*Sacrosanctum Concilium* (Vatican II, *Decree on the Liturgy* (1964) in Flannery 1975, 1–36)

Introduction

As with most liturgical books, the Lectionary is, for most people, most of the time, just there. Christians on a Sunday either hear passages taken from it, read from it, or preach upon its passages – depending on their ministries within the assembled people of God – and then devote attention to the passages rather than to the vehicle (i.e., the Lectionary) which selected those passages for that day. When the vehicle that lays out the readings does become the focus for attention it is usually for all the wrong reasons: why was *that* reading there today, who put that with that, why can we not have the beauty of that translation, or what was wrong with the old books that we ever changed? When the Lectionary comes to view in these situations it is already in the dock and on the defensive.

By contrast, this book is not focused on any one reading – and will try to avoid getting sidetracked into discussing particular choices or problematic readings – but will give its attention directly to the vehicle that brings us reading after reading, Sunday after Sunday. That vehicle, the Lectionary, is both complex and noble in its aspirations – and for both reasons is a worthy object of study in itself, not only by those who preside or preach at the liturgy but by all Christians who, when they assemble as a church, make use of it.

The Lectionary is not to be seen as just some complex book (and most liturgical books are complex and have the expectation that only experts need to find their way around them) – rather it is a deliberate attempt to bring the Scriptures in their totality into the life of the Church. It is the carefully planned programme to use the Scriptures as the primary elucidation of the great liturgical seasons, and to make the evangelists' own presentation of the person and ministry of Jesus the basis on which we encounter the memory of the Lord. Moreover, the liturgy is an event: a gathering of the baptized to express who they are as disciples, a celebration of the presence of Christ among them (Matt. 18.20), and the act of joining with him in offering praise and thanks to the Father. To read the Scriptures in this context is to perform an act of identification with one another as we share our central and common religious memories through listening together, but is also to engage in the action of remembering and proclaiming 'the mighty acts of [God] who called [us] out of darkness into his own marvellous light' (NRSV) and who as his 'holy nation' (1 Pet. 2.9) now bless and thank the Father.

Such a Lectionary as we have now – and it is a closely related family of liturgical arrangements covering most of the mainline Western churches, Catholic and Protestant – is something almost completely new in Christian history. There have been many lectionaries over the centuries, but that which emerged within the Catholic Church in the aftermath of the Second Vatican Council, and which provides the basic shape found in all the members of the current lectionary family, is unique in its scope, extent and arrangement. But while it has been in use now for more than 40 years, and has won many admirers among those who have responsibility for providing liturgical books within churches, it is still lacking in widespread appreciation – and often criticisms of it go unanswered through ignorance. My hope is that this book will win it new admirers, and help release its potential in our assemblies.[1]

---

[1] The Lectionary as used by the churches is a far larger phenomenon than the Lectionary for Sundays and the major festivals; however, it is this part of the Lectionary where both its greatest genius resides and it has its greatest impact, so this book will confine itself to this part of the Lectionary. Only when one has come to grips with this core, can one proceed to examine its less significant sections.

At the end of the book is a guide to further reading, and on particular points that readers might want to follow up I have placed references in brackets with this sign, >, which means: if you want to know more about this point, go to that book or article whose details are listed under 'Further reading'.

Part 1

BASIC QUESTIONS

1

Why do we read the Scriptures at the Eucharist?

Is this a question?

'Why read the Bible in church?' What a question! Is it not simply a 'given' that when we assemble as Christians, then we must read from the Scriptures? After all, did not even Jesus do it when he went to the synagogue on the Sabbath (Luke 4.16–30)? So ingrained is the notion that 'when we gather, then we read from the Bible' that this is one of the very few activities that can be found right across the Christian spectrum on any Sunday morning. At one end of the spectrum we can imagine a Pentecostal gathering with its band in a central position on a stage, but nearby will be a pulpit, lectern or reading desk with a Bible, while the worship leader will carry a Bible in his hand like a staff of office: reading from that book somehow underwrites the authority of the event. At the other end of the spectrum come the Catholic and Orthodox gatherings. Here the Mass, Eucharist or Divine Liturgy is the central and unvarying focus of Sunday, and it is the significance of the Eucharist, as such, that explains the significance of the gathering, yet the greatest part of the time is taken up with the reading of the Scriptures and their explanation in preaching (or, at least, that is supposed to be the focus of preaching). Almost no Catholic or Orthodox Christian would say that he or she attends the Eucharist for the readings, yet vast amounts of effort are expended in training clergy to lead this Liturgy of the Word.[1] If for many Catholics and Orthodox the readings are simply a preamble to 'the real business'

---

[1] Denominations vary in their use of 'Ministry of the Word' or 'Liturgy of the Word'; but whether they use a Latin-based word ('ministry') or a Greek-based one ('liturgy') is a matter of style – in each case they are referring to the same reality in worship. 'Liturgy of the Word' will be the term used here as it has the widest currency.

of Sunday, the Eucharist, then, by contrast, for many mainstream Protestant churches it is the reading and the preaching that have the primary place on a Sunday, and the less frequent Lord's Supper, or Holy Communion, is seen as somehow an addition to the normal weekly fare of the readings. But in every case, the reading of passages from the same collection, more or less, of ancient authors constitutes a central religious action and a focus for the community's gathering.

Moreover, in recent decades most Western churches with fixed liturgical forms (Catholics, Anglicans, Lutherans . . .) have revised their liturgies not just for the Eucharist but right across the board, and a feature of these revisions has been either an increase in the use of the Scriptures or the introduction of a Liturgy of the Word where there had not formerly been one. So, for example, until 1971 the Catholic liturgy of Baptism had no readings from Scripture, but today it has a Liturgy of the Word which, in structure, is identical to that at the Eucharist: Old Testament reading, Psalm, New Testament Letter, Gospel, Homily, before proceeding with the actual act of baptizing – and similar developments have taken place in many other churches. And for most Western churches, beginning with the Catholics in 1969, the volume of Scripture read each Sunday has increased, while the range of biblical material used in the whole cycle of liturgy has more than tripled. The result of these developments is this: *more use is being made of the Scriptures in worship today than at any time in the past two millennia.* But the fact that we all do this, and imagine we have always done this, does not explain why we do it.

How we set about answering this question will, in turn, reflect other aspects of our own personal theologies, revealing positions that often lurk, almost unrecognized, in the background of our attitudes to liturgy and to the biblical readings in our assemblies. Here are three very common explanations that one finds when one probes this question with Christians (and, to a large extent, it does not seem to matter whether or not they are laypeople or clergy).

'The Bible = God's revelation'

Is the Bible the actual revelation of God or is it a record of that revelation? This is a fundamental question: how we answer it will affect every aspect of how we approach the Scriptures. Many Christians imagine that the Bible is like God's 'instruction manual' for life and happiness, and that any historical details we recall in the stories in the book simply refer to what is the delivery mechanism for the sacred text. This approach has a long history in Christianity and its focus on 'the book' is reinforced by the fact that it allows apparently simple comparisons of the Christian message with that of other philosophies and religions. However, the mainline position within Christianity (and within Judaism) is that God has not given us a book, but revealed his love – and so his identity – in a series of mighty acts: choosing a people, delivering them from slavery, establishing a standing relationship ('the covenant') with them, guiding them by prophets, and showing his care in umpteen other ways. And for his followers, the advent of Jesus is the event that brings the other events to completion: he sets up a new relationship sealed in his own blood on the cross, and reveals in himself the inner life of God. These events are remembered by his people, and committed to writing: hence, these writings are the aide-memoire of the community founded in the divine actions.

For those who take the first approach – the Bible = what God wants us to know and believe – there is then little question about why we read whenever we gather: reading the Bible equals acquaintance with God. For them the question often becomes: why do anything else when we gather except listen (and perhaps have an expert explanation)? Or, if we are all literate, why not just let everyone read for themselves? It was a variant of this approach to the Bible that led many groups at the Reformation to abandon the notion of a weekly Eucharist in favour of gathering for listening to the Scriptures and to preaching. The reverse is also true: if you are gathering for the Eucharist, then you are already committed to a notion of revelation that is based in events remembered, and reading will then be a support to the act of recollection and the discovery of the significance of events. It is worth noting, however, that one of the tensions in any gathering for the Eucharist is that there will be those whose approach to the Bible is such that they cannot see the Lectionary's readings in the larger context of the eucharistic event which is actually taking place: the emphasis may be so placed on the readings, that the eucharistic meal comes to be regarded as just an afterthought. That said, in encountering the Scriptures we, through the Spirit, encounter the presence of God.

'We need teaching and a programme of teaching'

If you look at the shape of most older church buildings and a trad-itional classroom or lecture hall you will notice, immediately, certain similarities of organization and function. This is not accidental: the classroom is copied from the church; both are locations where a teacher imparts instruction to those who stand in need of it. And as the textbooks of maths, grammar or science instruct people in matters of earthly importance, so the textbooks in 'things divine' (the Scriptures) instruct us in the mysteries of the higher world. One set of books is studied in the classroom, the other in the chapel. This is a neat and convenient ordering of reality that can be traced back to the time of Cassiodorus (c.490–c.580) and has inspired monks and teachers ever since. It is a pattern that still can be found underlying many theology programmes, and it operates just under the surface for many clergy in the way they view the Scriptures. This approach sees the time of the readings as, in effect, a class for either teaching about the Scriptures, imparting their content, or using them as the basis for teaching the belief system of Christians.

The problem with this approach is that it is not clear how the readings constitute liturgy as distinct from having the 'school hour' attached to the 'worship hour'. Likewise, when teaching becomes the dominant note, it is not clear why we do not organize the readings around a teaching plan, or, at least, around clear themes. Moreover, while a Christian teacher might want to teach about Jesus or read Paul (always a favourite with those who focus on the readings as 'teaching'), it is not at all clear why we should read some of the Old Testament passages we find set out. For those who want to view the Liturgy of the Word as a class, there is often a great desire to omit or tidy up readings, or even to replace them with items that 'bring the theme out clearly'. So why, for this group, are there readings at the Eucharist? Because we need instruction and this is a convenient time for it. However, as we find the readings laid out for us in the Lectionary, they are seen as part of the worship of a community of believers, not as a class for carrying out either basic evangelization or catechetical instruction. That said, whenever the Scriptures are read, and preaching takes place, there is a dimension of teaching or formation to the event, and we have to reckon with this as well as recognizing that the practice of liturgy (i.e., doing what the community does when it is together) should be a key way of learning what is involved in a life of discipleship.

'We need some inspiration and reflection in our lives'

We need to be recalled to the great truths, we need to set our lives in perspective, we need the calming effect of some philosophy and the vision of the 'big picture'. When can we get this 'inspiration'? When we gather for an hour's calm and reflection on a Sunday morning: this should be a time to think good thoughts and refresh ourselves! The homily, consequently, should not be expository but 'something to take away' – a 'thought for the day'. If the second approach – the Liturgy of the Word is a Bible class or a period of doctrinal instruction – tends to be an attitude very common among leaders of worship, then the notion that the readings should be inspirational 'food for the soul' tends to be found among those who are not ministers. The position is a deeply problematic one in that it applies to liturgy (literally: the public service of God) a consumerist view of Sunday morning: I join the gathering for what it gives me, what I can take away from it, and one wonders whether or not these 'wants' could be better fulfilled by some Sunday morning radio programme with a reflective tone, which would also allow us to avoid the disquiet of having to gather, interact, and sit in an uncomfortable pew! 'Some people go to church to get spirituality, but I get it walking in the park' is emblematic of this consumerist approach, and many who actually gather share the approach but simply substitute the source: they expect it from what they hear – but this often subjects the liturgy to a test (i.e., to supply my want for some 'spirituality') which it will very often fail. Liturgical gatherings exist so that we can remember – an activity covering the whole of the liturgy and not just the readings – and on the basis of remembering, give thanks to the Father in and through Jesus.

However, there will be many people in any congregation that believe the readings are there for enlightenment and inspiration, yet they may find they are disappointed more often than not. Many of the Old Testament readings will simply generate a 'So what?' response, while Paul's concerns about the self-understanding of the early churches – with the exception of 1 Corinthians 12.31—13.13 – may seem 'irrelevant'. The Gospels might seem a better bet because of the widespread notion that they contain the 'wise words of Jesus', but some of the parables (e.g. Matt. 20.1–16) simply seem unjust and irritating. So while the notion of 'readings are there to inspire us' is a common justification of a Liturgy of the Word, it is one that does not long survive the test of reality. That said, it should be the concern of every minister that, through the Liturgy of the Word, discipleship is nourished and the gathering helped to proceed along its pilgrimage of faith.

Yet, when we think about our gatherings – be it for a Eucharist or for a Baptism – there is no reason, intrinsic to the event for which we have assembled, why we should have readings! The Eucharist is, at its core, a gathering for a meal, a meal which, for all the added layers of significance, is an event in itself when the disciples express their identity in Jesus, continue his meal practice, and express their joy at being 'called . . . out of darkness into [God's] marvellous light' (1 Pet. 2.9 NRSV). Eucharist, as the name implies, is the action of blessing and thanking the Father, in and through Jesus, in the action of sharing a loaf and cup for all that he has done and especially 'for the life and knowledge which [he has] made known to us' (*Didache* 9.3). Within such a meal of thanksgiving to the Father there is no reason why we should gather to listen to readings prior to gathering around the table! Moreover, in neither of the two earliest references (1 Corinthians and the *Didache*) to this gathering – both of which presuppose a real meal of all the followers of Jesus in a particular place – is there any hint of a synagogue-like assembly beforehand at which 'the Scriptures' (i.e., what we call the 'Old Testament') were read (> O'Loughlin 2010, 85–104). Similarly, in none of the remembered meals of Jesus – as recounted in the Gospels – or other early references to the meal (e.g. Acts 2.42, 46; Jude 12) is there any reference to a period of readings. It might be objected that the meal in Emmaus is an exception, when the risen Lord explained the Scriptures to them: but this was seen as a unique event and it is presented as taking place *after* the moment of recognition at the breaking of the loaf (Luke 24.13–35). Likewise, some have sought to explain readings at the Eucharist by parallel with the stories recalled at a Passover meal. But this fails to notice that the Eucharist was from the beginning a weekly celebration modelled on the Sabbath-eve meal and the 'grace' that was uttered at that meal. The *explanation* of the

Eucharist in terms of the Passover (as found in Mark 14.14) is a later development.

So we are left with the fact that the 'Meal of Thanksgiving', as such, does not need to have a service of readings, but for most of Christian history, and for all communities today, it has been preceded by a period of reading, preaching and intercessory prayer. Equally, while we could imagine a situation where the celebration of the Lord's message took place at a different time from the celebration of the Lord's banquet, in the actual world of Christian customs there is always a Liturgy of the Word before any other action of the community.

This invariable practice has two consequences. First, there is often a tension between the sense of joy that is inherent within the community's 'Banquet of Thanksgiving', celebrating the resurrection each Sunday, and the tone of the readings on a particular Sunday. The fact is this: while the liturgy of Baptism will have readings deliberately chosen to provide background to the event, this will not normally be the case at the Eucharist. We have, in effect, two distinct elements joined to one another, each of which has its own integrity and each of which is precious in our view of Christian life. We live with this tension and we address it in many of the variable prayers – such as the variety of Prefaces and Eucharistic Prayers – which seek to link the readings of the day with the fact that we are gathered for the Eucharist. The prayers do this by linking the meal – which has over centuries generated a feast of meanings – to being thankful for some particular aspect of the mystery of Christ such as we might have heard about in the readings. So not only must we acknowledge this tension, but be attentive to the need to draw the Liturgy of the Word and the Liturgy of the Eucharist together so that they form a single celebration at the actual gathering.

Second, the constant presence of the readings prior to the actual gathering at the Lord's Table has led Christians to see in this pattern a reflection of a theological truth: we can only celebrate the event of the presence of the Lord's Anointed in our lives, be it in Baptism or the Eucharist, in so far as we have already heard his word and have chosen to respond in faith. So just as someone will only seek baptism after having heard the gospel, or seek to join in the eucharistic meal after having accepted the gospel, so a moment of announcement (the Liturgy of the Word) should precede the sacramental event (be it

Baptism or the Eucharist). While this is a convenient theological link, and, indeed, expresses a theological truth, it is a reflection based on the facts of Christian practice rather than the master plan that underpins practice. Because it is reflection on practice, it is best not to push the analogy too far as an explanation: after all, Christians are seeking to live an ongoing life of growing discipleship, which involves listening out for the word of God, and a part of discipleship is regularly gathering for the Christian meal. Trying to imagine this ongoing life in terms of an 'act of hearing' followed neatly by an 'act of thanking' is simply untrue to the continuity that is at the core of human existence.

How did the Liturgy of the Word at a gathering for the Eucharist originate?

So if we can find no explanation for readings at the Eucharist through an analysis of the actions of 'listening' and 'thanking', was it the sheer convenience of 'getting it all done in one session' that led the Christians to combine the elements that we can distinguish in terms of their nature? We can only appreciate why we have readings at our weekly gathering by approaching the issue from a completely different angle. The first 'churches' (literally: 'gatherings') were made up in the main of Jewish disciples whose core belief was that the only true God had established a relationship ('the covenant') with them. This covenant constituted them as 'his people', gave them their identity and their way of life. For them to know who they were and what they were about was to recall that covenant: so remembering, recalling, was at the heart of knowing God. The prophets can be seen as those who recalled Israel to this identity, and to participate in that covenant was to share in that memory. To understand this we need to think of memory and identity, history and living not as separate categories (a very modern division) but as forming a circle. To be the people God wanted them to be now required recalling the past, the past gave explanations and structure to the present, and, indeed, the future with its hopes (e.g. deliverance) and fears (e.g. the various apocalyptic movements announcing that judgement was nigh). When Henry Ford declared that 'history is bunk' or someone says that the 'past is prologue', they are expressing the modern Western attitude to history; but this contemporary view of the past is radically different from that of Judaism at the time of Jesus (and indeed from virtually all religious traditions).

If someone were to ask Jesus, or any of his fellow Jews, about his beliefs, the answer would not take the form of an abstract doctrinal plan, but a history lesson: I am who I am because of these events long ago which are not just background but explain my inmost identity. That memory was the common possession of all who shared it, and it was recorded in writing: 'the Scriptures'.

So before we can look at anything connected to the Liturgy of the Word we need to recall this loop, illustrated in Figure 1.

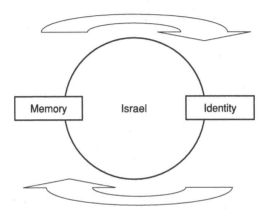

Figure 1

Memory gave shape to life, and life was lived within an understanding shaped by memory. This memory was not simply the books that make up our canon of the Old Testament, but was the living community memory of the great events that make us who we are. It included those texts we call the Old Testament, many texts that they thought of as equal to it but that we no longer read (e.g., *1 Enoch* is quoted as Scripture in Jude 14), and many other texts besides. But these texts lived by being performed as part of the oral culture of worship in the Temple, the synagogue – where the first lectionaries evolved (> Aageson 1992) – and the home, and that memory was augmented and made present in any number of interpersonal encounters. The canonical books were 'the classics' of that memory, and the more any event could be seen within their reinterpretation, the more it made sense within their everyday lives. We see this process of reading within cultural or ritual memory, and then that memory being used to inform the present in the incident of Jesus reading from the

Book of Isaiah, in the synagogue on a Sabbath gathering, and then declaring: 'Today this scripture has been fulfilled in your hearing' (Luke 4.16–21 NRSV).

We live in a culture of the *written* word[2] – just think what you are doing as you read this: you are engaging in deciphering signs which communicate my thoughts to you without ever a sound being uttered – and this culture of reading has been with us since the educational revolution of Hugh of St Victor (d. 1142) at the dawn of scholasticism (> Illich 1993). Before that time – and the question is more complex than simply the extent of education and literacy – people lived in an oral culture: *books were records of speech*, and an oral culture is also an *aural* culture: one learns with one's ears by listening – even when one looks at the marks on the page with one's eyes, one turns them into sounds and these are heard (> Achtemeier 1990). This information may seem a long way from making sense of the Lectionary but bear in mind the following two points.

First, Paul says that 'faith comes from what is heard' (Rom. 10.17 NRSV): it is a good idea to look up in a concordance the number of times that 'hearing' is seen as the basis of receiving the gospel (> O'Loughlin 2007a). However, in our culture we tend to privilege, for serious matters, the act of reading, usually alone, as the way to knowledge: but the message of Judaism, and then of the followers of Jesus, was not one of books but of *speech*, and speech could, at times, be recorded and stored in books. It was a religion of the spoken word, heard and remembered, not piety based in a library.

Second, on any Sunday morning right across the world today there will be someone at a lectern reading texts aloud: turning words stored in marks on paper back into sounds. But in many places virtually everyone at the gathering can read, and very often will be following the reading in their own books, or on service sheets, reading silently! Does that not seem strange? We all have done it, and will continue to do it, but stop and think how silly the scene is: there is all the fuss of reading aloud, yet many being read to by the lector are not listening, but reading the very same text for themselves. It might, indeed, be less distracting to have us all read the appropriate passage in the books

---

[2] For an introduction to how the culture of the printed book informed our religious perception, > McLuhan 1962.

provided in silence. So why do we carry on with the practice of public reading? The common answer is that this is a hangover from the time when few could read and books were expensive; but actually it is a practice that goes back to the aural culture in which those books were produced. Our intellectual culture changed, but not our ritual practice. Ritual is conservative: therefore people continued to behave as they had always done, despite the fact that they preferred to study the text by reading it silently. But unlike this book, written with an individual reader in mind, ancient books were composed to be heard when read aloud, and we lose a great deal when we forget that.

All ancient books were composed within an aural culture, and fed a culture of memory, and each time they were read has to be seen as a performance rather than a moment of private reading (> Smith 2001). The reading of a passage from one of the Scriptures is more akin to hearing a singer perform a well-loved song than a moment of textual study (such as you are engaged in now as you read this). So we are actually engaged in a performance of our memory at our gatherings for the Lord's meal on a Sunday. And, thought of in this way, we can see how the Liturgy of the Word became an invariable element in the festive gatherings of the early groups of the disciples of Jesus (> Bradshaw 2009, 3–52).

Every gathering of the disciples of Jesus – it would be inaccurate to designate them as 'Christians' (implying a distinct religion from Judaism) at this stage – was an affirmation of their identity and memory. These gatherings at which they continued Jesus' meal practice of 'blessing the Father' (which was equivalent to 'offering him thanks') were the primary community actions of remembering him ('do this in memory of me' in 1 Cor. 11.24, 25) and of identification with him (1 Cor. 10.16–31; and > Taussig 2009). So when any apostle, or travelling teacher, or evangelist happened to be in a gathering (we get the details regarding the welcome accorded to these in *Didache* 11–13), it would be natural that some of the training in ways of discipleship would take place at the same time as the festive meal which celebrated the presence of the Christ among them. We get echoes of this in the Acts of the Apostles in the references to Paul joining in meal gatherings in houses where it is clear that he was teaching, but equally clear that all were celebrating the Lord's Supper. Here is the account of what happened after Paul landed in Troas: 'On the first day of the week, when we were gathered together to break bread, Paul talked with them, intending to depart on the morrow; and he prolonged his speech until midnight' (Acts 20.7 RSV). And then 'when Paul had gone up and had broken bread and eaten, he conversed with them a long while, until daybreak, and so departed' (Acts 20.11 RSV). Luke, in presenting Paul as a teacher visiting churches, presents the event of his visit as taking place at that church's meal. This means that by the time Luke wrote Acts (late first or early second century) the pattern of performing the memory of Jesus in words on the same occasions when it was performed in the Breaking of the Loaf was already an established one.

We have a curious confirmation of this as the standard pattern in a letter Pliny (the Younger) wrote, as governor of Bithynia (south coast of the Black Sea), to the emperor Trajan around AD 112. Asked to investigate the goings on of the 'Christians', he wrote:

> the Christians said [when I interrogated them] that the worst thing they had done was this: that their custom was to meet on a chosen day before dawn and to sing, between themselves, a song to 'Christ' as to one of the gods, and to commit themselves formally by oath, not for any wicked deed, but to avoid theft, robbery, adultery, and false dealings. After this ceremony ended they usually departed and then met again to take food, but it was ordinary and harmless food, and they ceased this after I had promulgated your imperial order banning secret societies.[3]

Pliny was neither an anthropologist nor a student of religious ritual, so we do not get a nuanced account of Christian activities, but it is clear that there was a celebration in words and singing, and then a celebration with food.

Since we find this pattern of a celebration of the memory in words followed by the meal in all directions in early Christianity, the pattern must be very early indeed. Thus we find it in all the ancient references to the liturgy to the south in Egypt and Ethiopia; to the east in Syria and Mesopotamia; to the north in Greece; and to the west in the Latin-speaking lands. But for all its crassness, Pliny's description is our first explicit confirmation of the pattern. Soon the pattern would be formalized into the shape, more or less, in which we have

---

[3] Letter 47 (all translations, unless otherwise noted, are my own); for Latin text, > Sherwin-White 1969, 68–70; for whole text in English, > Bettenson 1963, 3–4.

it. Within a few decades – with all the apostles long dead and even those who knew them no longer around in churches – Justin, about AD 150 (> Parvis 2008), could write thus:

> On the day called Sunday we hold a community assembly . . . and the memoirs of the apostles or the writings of the prophets are read for as long as there is time. Then when the reader has finished, the leader of the assembly encourages us to imitate the example of what we have heard. Then we all stand up and offer up our petitions, and when these prayers are finished, a loaf and wine and water are presented . . .[4]

Justin was trying to explain Christian practice to the larger society, which had little understanding of this new religion, and chose this phrase 'memoirs of the apostles' (he used it on many occasions in his writings) because it would be readily intelligible in a way that the word 'Gospel' as used by Christians would not be (> Stanton 2004, 92–105). But note that he does not say 'books about' as we would; rather he thinks of the readings as taking the place of the memories of the people, the apostles, who were commissioned by Jesus to spread his good news. For Justin, this reading at a gathering was not a group studying a book, but a re-enactment of memory by a reader; it was a performance that placed those *listening* in the presence of the apostolic preaching.

So why do we have readings? Because the memory manifested in the readings identifies us for who we are – disciples – and celebrates the presence of the Christ whom we recognize in terms of an even longer memory: Israel's covenant. But this is not in the least easy for us to appreciate today. It is based within an attitude to religious identity that is alien to us.

- We see religious identity in terms of belief 'making sense within our lives', not on the basis of a history to which we belong. Yet we read texts that give us details of a society several millennia ago.
- We tend to look on the books of the Scriptures as either divine oracles or treatises rather than as 'frozen memories' which we repeat and reinterpret. Yet they are performed liturgically as part of a communal celebration, not as part of an adult education class.

---

[4] *First Apology* 67.

- We live in a culture of private reading rather than one where communal performance is seen as the road to growth in understanding and wisdom. Yet we still read these texts aloud just as we did long before the rise of modern culture.

All in all, the issue of having public, communal readings from the Scriptures each Sunday is far more complex than we usually imagine, and the persistence of the practice should raise many questions about how we understand our links to the past, to the Bible, and to worship (> West 1997, 3–11).

Why read from the Gospels?

Justin often referred to the Gospels as 'the memoirs of the apostles' and the term has much to recommend it. Many people today when asked about the Gospels would use terms like 'the biography of Jesus' or 'Jesus' teaching', hoping by such a phrase to outline their content. Justin's phrase, by contrast, emphasizes that these are what a specific community, the apostles, within the larger community of disciples *remembered* about Jesus; and memory is about what is significant and what is kept with you, rather than listing the details in the fashion of a set of annals. Those who knew Jesus made sense of him through the history they already held dear as part of the community living within a covenant with God; and, in turn, they believed in Jesus because they saw him and his life, and death, in relation to the history of that covenant. Their history made sense of Jesus and Jesus made sense of their history (see Figure 2).

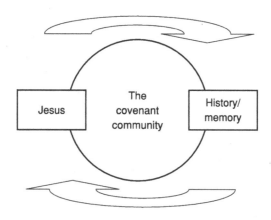

Figure 2

It was this understanding that was transmitted in the preaching of the apostles in the first gatherings, and we see Luke's recognition of this structure in his idealized first sermon by Peter in Jerusalem on the Day of Pentecost:

Men of Judea and all who live in Jerusalem, let this be known to you, and listen to what I say . . . this is what was spoken through the prophet Joel:

'In the last days it will be, God declares, that I will pour out my Spirit upon all flesh, and your sons and your daughters shall prophesy, and your young men shall see visions, and your old men shall dream dreams. . . . Then everyone who calls on the name of the Lord shall be saved.'

You that are Israelites, listen to what I have to say: Jesus of Nazareth, a man attested to you by God with deeds of power, wonders, and signs that God did through him among you, as you yourselves know – this man, handed over to you according to the definite plan and fore-knowledge of God, you crucified and killed by the hands of those outside the law. But God raised him up, having freed him from death, because it was impossible for him to be held in its power.

For David says concerning him, 'I saw the Lord always before me, for he is at my right hand so that I will not be shaken; . . . For you will not abandon my soul to Hades, or let your Holy One experience corruption . . . you will make me full of gladness with your presence.'

Fellow Israelites, I may say to you confidently of our ancestor David that he both died and was buried, and his tomb is with us to this day. Since he was a prophet, he knew that God had sworn with an oath to him that he would put one of his descendants on his throne. Foreseeing this, David spoke of the resurrection of the Messiah, saying, 'He was not abandoned to Hades, nor did his flesh experience corruption.'

This Jesus God raised up, and of that all of us are witnesses. Being therefore exalted at the right hand of God, and having received from the Father the promise of the Holy Spirit, he has poured out this that you both see and hear. For David did not ascend into the heavens, but he himself says, 'The Lord said to my Lord, "Sit at my right hand, until I make your enemies your footstool."'

Therefore let the entire house of Israel know with certainty that God has made him both Lord and Messiah, this Jesus whom you crucified. (Acts 2.14–36 NRSV)

What is fascinating about this carefully constructed speech is the repeated circularity of past and present: what was said obscurely by Joel (2.16) was now manifest in the present. The audience are twice addressed as 'Israelites' (2.22, 29) – their ancient covenant name – and urged to act now; and David is invoked three times (2.25, 31, 34) to the effect that he identifies Jesus, while Jesus makes clear what David was speaking about as a prophet. Thus, out of the richness of their historical identity they can finally confess that Jesus has been made Lord and Christ (Messiah) in the final sentence of the speech. This circularity, though often we are barely conscious of its presence, underpins all the Gospels, which *remember* the events and words relating to Jesus. Or as John put it: 'But these are written so that you may come to believe that Jesus is the Messiah, the Son of God, and that through believing you may have life in his name' (John 20.31 NRSV).

So when the Gospels are formally proclaimed in the assembly, it is this original sense of the proclamation which makes Jesus present that is at work. The Gospel is not read either as a headline to form the basis of teaching (i.e., the way I have just used the quotation from Acts) nor as a reminder of some core ideas about Christian faith or where we have come from; rather, in the liturgy, *the Gospel is a performance of the presence of Jesus*, acknowledged as Lord and Christ in this community. They do this now through an act of communal recollection – hence all are listening to one voice rather than being individuals reading their own books – which re-enacts his presence in the way that apostles, his witnesses, spoke in the first gatherings.

This view of the Gospels as enacting presence, performances of memories that break down the separations of space and time, is at the heart of their use in the liturgy. But we should note that this is very different either from the way that we view the Gospels as historical documents or the way that we use them in many other religious contexts. Therefore we need to keep in mind that what we say about the Gospels when we try to describe them as 'objects' (i.e., texts) is different from what we say about them when describing their use as part of eucharistic worship. Because of these radically different perspectives – which can fruitfully be seen as complementary to one another but which are often simply confused or reduced to one or other – it is a useful task for anyone involved with the readings in the liturgy to jot down and think about what she or he thinks 'the gospel' means, what 'a Gospel' is, and what a reading from 'the Gospel' (by one of four authors) is at the liturgy.

Why read from the Old Testament?

While few Christians would find the reading of the Gospels (however they understand the action) problematic, many find reading passages from the Old Testament incomprehensible. On the other hand, there are those who cannot see what the fuss is about: is not one passage from the Bible just as good as another? Therefore, how one approaches this question can expose a great deal about how we understand revelation. However, before looking at that question, we should address the two most commonly expressed arguments.

The first is based on an 'appeal to relevance' and takes the form 'who in my congregation wants to know about "the Canaanites, the Hittites, the Hivites, the Perizzites, the Girgashites, the Amorites, and the Jebusites" (Josh. 3.10 RSV)?' This may be the simple truth: no one wants to waste their time on this text they think of as irrelevant, obscure and of no value to them. We now speak openly of 'consuming media' and in our culture anything communicated must be fast, 'touch me', and be easily digested. There is no simple answer to this assault despite many attempts to recreate the whole of the liturgy around some aspect of contemporary culture (> Spinks 2010). But we should note that if we apply our approach to consuming media consistently, then the whole notion of worship becomes redundant. Liturgy is not a product to be consumed, but a desire to act with others in a community to praise God and to image among ourselves the world revealed by faith.

The second common criticism of the Old Testament, and this is one heard mainly from clergy, is that it raises complexities and difficulties in a way that the New Testament readings, apparently, do not. Making sense of the legacy of faith and seeking to communicate with others about faith are among the most complex of human tasks. It is an illusion to imagine that it is simpler to make sense of a Gospel passage than any other: there are always difficulties – which is why so much effort is expended on training people in exegesis – and the situation is not helped by simply ignoring part of our legacy. The Old Testament's books have played a major role in making Christianity what it is, and we simply cannot cut it adrift. That said, the support that many clergy receive on an ongoing basis is in many churches derisory. When any scheme to support ministers is being prepared and a list of 'wants' is drawn up, it is very rare that any item to help with making use of the Old Testament – despite its place virtually every Sunday in the central act of worship – survives until the published programme.

More significant is the criticism that the Old is 'old hat' (now that we have the New) or some simple 'before–after' notions which contrast 'the Old Testament God' (usually not a nice notion) with 'the New Testament God' (usually an attractive notion). This sort of assault – and it can be found as early as the second century – simply ignores the nature of the gospel as it took shape among the apostles. The loop that can be seen in the formation of the Gospels still affects us: one can only appreciate the Gospels on the basis of the memory of the existing covenant whose memory is kept alive for us by, among other things, our reading of the books of the Old Testament. If one cannot try to appropriate the memory that animated the first disciples, then one cannot appreciate why they acclaimed Jesus 'as Lord and Christ'.

The foundation of the Newer Covenant is the Older Covenant: the Old is the basis, context, and key to the New. Hence, contrasts of the 'Old = bad/New = good' type must be strenuously avoided.[5] We need to remember that without a familiarity with those Scriptures the Christian religion can easily become, as it often has, a cult of 'the teachings of Jesus'. After all, we echo the early Christians when we confess in the Nicene Creed that Jesus rose on the third day 'in accordance with the scriptures' (see 1 Cor. 15.3, 4), and the very Scriptures in question are those we refer to as the Old Testament.

By contrast, the approach that sees little difference between one chunk of text and another – provided both are taken from the Bible – fails to grasp the nature of the Gospels' relationship to the past in the opposite direction. The gospel preached by the apostles, the kerygma, was that history points to Jesus and Jesus brought a long history to completion. We see this claim in Paul's notion of 'the

---

[5] These comparisons come in many forms: from the truly awful (as when 'the Old Testament God' is seen as somehow different from 'the New Testament God') to the simply misleading (as when someone refers to the Old Testament as 'out of date' and the New as 'in date') – all such comparisons negate the very basis on which we acclaim Jesus as 'the anointed one'.

fullness of time' in Galatians 4.4–5: 'But when the time had fully come, God sent forth his Son, born of woman, born under the law, to redeem those who were under the law, so that we might receive adoption as sons' (RSV); we see it in early statements about Jesus being the 'Alpha and Omega' (e.g. Rev. 21.6); and in the genealogies in Matthew's and Luke's Gospels. While the memory was necessary to make sense of Jesus, he was seen as the key to history and its culmination. So, once any Jew had opted to become a follower of Jesus, Jesus became the lens through which the whole of the memory (which included the Scriptures) was seen. To treat the whole of the Bible as just a bag from which one can pull out bits – allowing that it is a very common approach – does not do justice to the nature of Christian faith as it was handed on by the apostles. Luke makes this view explicit at Emmaus: 'Then beginning with Moses and all the prophets, he interpreted to them the things about himself in all the scriptures' (Luke 24.27 NRSV).

Why read from the early Christian letters?

Within 20 years of the death of Jesus there were gatherings of disciples not just in places where Jesus preached, but wherever Jews had settled – and perhaps already even beyond those areas. These churches formed a network that took advantage of good sea and road communications (> Thompson 1998) and between them travelled apostles, evangelists, prophets and teachers (> O'Loughlin 2010, 105–28). We know only a handful of the names of this group, and one stands out: Paul. We see from his letters and from the later memory of him in Acts that he travelled from church to church, and that he not only carried out his teaching with his own voice when he was present but by letter (> 1 Thess. 5.27). The arrival of a letter, which could be turned back into sound by a skilled reader, was Paul's virtual presence in these gatherings (> 2 Thess. 2.15; 2 Cor. 2.11). Moreover, just as the teachers moved from church to church, so too did the letters: 'and when this letter has been read among you, have it read also in the church of the Laodiceans; and see that you read also the letter from Laodicea' (Col. 4.16 NRSV).

These letters addressed both the nature of discipleship and the local questions of the day, and 20 of them – those we still use in the liturgy – are to be found in the canon of the New Testament (although that collection actually contains more letters, in that what we possess and read is an early edition of the letters that has, in places, embedded one letter within another). Alongside these we have about a dozen other early letters – some older than those in the canonical collection – that were circulated among the early churches. The pattern of reading letters at the weekly gathering (> Acts 20.7) in lieu of absent teachers has continued ever since. Indeed, until 1970, in many Christian churches using lectionaries the only readings on a Sunday were a section from an apostolic letter ('the epistle') and one from a Gospel (> Appendix 6). However, despite the antiquity of the practice, these readings are often the most difficult to understand partly because one often needs to know the whole letter to make sense of a part, and partly because what was often a burning issue of the day in the first communities is not an issue for us; yet the antiquity of the practice and the place of honour that is attached to the letters of Paul in Christian culture and theology often means that we feel we cannot simply drop the letter from the liturgy, but equally can do little (in the confines of worship) to make a passage less opaque.

Why sing psalms?

If the books of the Old Testament were the formalized history of the people, then within that history the collections of Psalms had a special place as hymns and songs, many sung time and again in worship (> Mowinckel 1962). If we think for a moment about how the traditional hymns of any Christian church have shaped its common memory, we can appreciate how such sung poetry can root itself in human memory in a most profound way. We can, therefore, imagine the Psalms as 'the hymnbook of Israel'. That hymnbook was made up not just of the 150 or so[6] psalms of the Book of Psalms, but of other pieces of poetry (some of which are found in our biblical books: Isa. 42.10–16, for example); and collectively they formed

---

[6] There are problems with numbering the Psalms, for some were sung in some places as two separate psalms, in others as single psalms – and the various number systems used today (one based on the ancient Greek translation for the Jews of the Mediterranean world, the other based on a later Hebrew text) reflect this varied usage. This is why still today different churches use different numberings of the Psalms (see Appendix 7).

in the communal memory a language for speaking about God and his promises. We can see this use of a common stock of images for speaking about God in the way Luke uses several quotations from the Psalms in Peter's sermon at the beginning of Acts. The first followers of Jesus, quite naturally, continued their community's use of this body of hymnody, and, as with the rest of the Old Testament, used this memory in their process of making sense of the event of Jesus as the Christ.

This continuity of use of the existing body of hymnody can be seen in the incidental references to psalms or hymns in early documents. Thus Paul wrote: 'When you come together, each one has a hymn, a lesson, a revelation, a tongue, or an interpretation. Let all things be done for edification' (1 Cor. 14.26 RSV). While in Paul's name, another writes that they should be 'addressing one another in psalms and hymns and spiritual songs, singing and making melody to the Lord with all your heart' (Eph. 5.19 RSV); and Mark concludes his account of the Last Supper with 'and when they had sung a hymn, they went out to the Mount of Olives' (Mark 14.26 RSV) – which probably implies that the eucharistic gatherings of his time (the late 60s) ended with a hymn, and this would have been either a psalm or similar to one of the hymns we find embedded in early texts (e.g. Eph. 1.3–10 or Col. 1.12–20). However, it is the use of the psalms in the way Luke uses them in Peter's speech that lies behind the liturgical tradition: the psalms are taken to reflect the Old Testament's memory, in a different register, and then to enable the gospel to be understood. When Pliny recorded that the Christians 'sang songs to Christ as to one of the gods', it was probably a psalm that he had heard sung. Whether or not they can function in that way today is one of the more problematic questions we shall have to look at later in this book.

Performance: the past made present

The Liturgy of the Word at the Eucharist follows a pattern that we have seen can be traced back to the first-century practice of gatherings for their common meal of the disciples of Jesus. For them, the Old Testament was living memory and it was within that living memory that the event of the life, death and resurrection of Jesus was located. This memory was the possession of the people whose understanding of their history was, as Luke points out in his Pentecost scene, animated by the gift of the Spirit. This memory was enacted and performed when they met, aided and enhanced by teachers and prophets, and cherished in the living voices of the apostles and evangelists. As time passed the immediacy of that living voice receded and was replaced by the recordings of those voices in the form of books read aloud – and in the first half of the second century we can hear Bishop Papias say how he still preferred to hear from those who had a living contact through voice with the memory rather than from those who only heard it from recordings of voices stored in the form of writing in a book (> Hill 2006)!

By contrast, we think of 'the book' – the holy book – as a fundamental reality in religion, and we forget that Jesus is unusual among founders of religions in that he never wrote a book. However, if we are to appreciate the Liturgy of the Word, and make sense of the lectionaries that support it, then we have to set alongside that modern attitude one that belongs to the oral/aural world in which the gospel was preached. Jesus entrusted his message to a community, a community with a rich memory, and the memory of Jesus became the centre around which their whole memory and identity came to revolve. So we have to think of the readings at the Eucharist in terms of a community and its memories, and this memory – in which we encounter the Lord – is activated by the performance of that memory, that restatement of identity, that is the readings. We are not 'a people of the book' as we often so glibly say, but the community of the memory of Jesus as Lord and Christ. And that community has books whose oral performance – in the manner in which they were originally written – activates that memory while the Spirit gives it life.

2

What is a Gospel?

When listening to the Gospel at a Sunday Eucharist it might seem silly to ask what a Gospel is – it would appear to be obvious. But a moment's thought shows that this is not the case. For one thing, we might think of them as biographies of Jesus, but they are far from that. We might think of them as attempts to bring us to belief in Jesus, but they are not apologetic. Likewise, they are not instructions on how to live one's life, but they do contain teaching. And, while we think of them as the inspired accounts of Jesus, there is no end of difficulties in trying to bring them into some sort of historical alignment. So is there a better way to approach the question: what is a Gospel?

Whenever we encounter a Gospel passage we need to recall that it invites us to interact with it on six *interconnected* levels.

1 form
2 audience
3 story
4 history
5 myth
6 task.

These six levels are present, to a large extent, in every religious document, and they call forth a diversity of answers. Furthermore, they open us to a deeper level of questions about whether we accept the document as worthy of belief and acceptance. However, if we try to short-circuit these levels (as happens more often than not) we can end up in either an unthinking biblical fundamentalism or a similarly unthinking rejection of the Gospels. Therefore, before we go any further, we should bear two points in mind.

First, human beings have a bad habit of thinking that important information will be very simple in form. This is an attractive illusion because there are some very basic items of communication where this is true. Take the notice 'Danger: Hot Surface', for example. Here there is little or no ambiguity, a minimum amount of structure – just three words – and the effect desired is very clear: a warning. Take the even simpler communication of the stop sign on a road: this is a commandment that does not need interpretation or experts – you just obey it, or else! There are many who imagine that God either does or should communicate in this way, but they might be less enthusiastic if we asked them to describe themselves completely in just one simple sentence. Life is complex and mystery is manifold: the religious texts in which we seek to communicate about the divine to one another are always many layered.

Second, there is a curious, unspoken alignment between those biblical fundamentalists who want to accept the book on their own terms and those who attack religion on the basis of ridiculing sacred books. Both want to determine on their own terms, in a clinical abstract fashion, what would constitute the modes of revelation. Sacred Scripture, therefore, operates as they say it should operate, and then it supports their view of what should be: either there is a God, formed according to their principles, who has produced the books, and it is all very simple; or there is no being matching what they say God should be, so the books are nonsense, and it is all very simple.

Approaching the Gospels with the above set of six questions makes it all more complex, but it facilitates a reflective approach to some of the basic questions about belief that are thrown up by any religion that uses sacred texts.

Form

Every human product that communicates between us has a form: think of the difference between a lecture, a homily, a 'thought for the day' on the radio, or a brief question-and-answer session. When we look at the Gospels we see that they start at one time, then follow an individual day after day, and then move on to death (all four Gospels) and after death (Matthew, Luke and John). This form is the narrative of a life over time. Time's movement, and an individual life, are what give structure to the text. We today meet this structure when we read a biography, an obituary, or an encyclopaedia entry when we need 'to look someone up'. So can we say that the Gospels are biographies? Yes, in terms of 'form' (a life following the sequence of time) but not in terms of 'task' (because usually the task of a modern biography is to give us behind-the-scenes glimpses of the individual or to probe that person's motivations and influences for the decisions she or he took in life).

It is worth noting that the first generations of Christians (our Gospels were written between the late 60s and the early years of the second century) used many forms in their literature: biography in the Gospels, the form of a letter in the writings of Paul and several others, that of history in Acts, that of a training manual in the *Didache*, that of a vision in Revelation, and within these documents we have other forms such as hymns (e.g. Eph. 1.3–10). It is important to remember this variety of form (and there are others) for it reminds us that we have to encounter them in different ways. In other words, we must not approach them as 'one sack, one sample' because they are 'all in the Bible'. Just as one respects the difference in what may be said in a personal email and in a formal report, so we must respect the forms each document's creator chose. Given that we have four Gospels in the canon (three of them very similar) and fragments of many others, we can say that this was a very popular form in the churches. By contrast, we know that there were collections of the sayings of Jesus without this biographical form, but they did not survive in such quantity or popularity that they were later canonized. Their disappearance is easily explained: we all like following a narrative, the ups and downs of a life, especially one with a good storyline – and the four Gospels fit these criteria, but the *Gospel of Thomas* (which almost disappeared) does not.

Audience

In every communication we make certain assumptions about *who* is going to receive it and *how* they are going to receive it. There are some things that are best done on television, others that are best done in a book; some things can be said in an email and some need to be heard in person; a film of a play or book is very different from a live performance of the play or reading the book slowly over several days. A lecture makes assumptions about the level of interest, backgrounds and attention spans of students that are very different from a sermon, or a one-minute slot that will be broadcast and heard by people who might know little (or nothing) about the subject.

The Gospels were intended to be *heard*, not read, by people who were *already disciples* of Jesus and who were gathering regularly with the community. They were not intended as introductions for people curious about the new religion, nor for preaching in the marketplace to see if someone might join the group. Most ancient writings were intended to be heard, rather than be read silently as we read texts today. So we should think of these writings as more akin to a recording of someone's speech sent through the post, rather than as a variant on a modern book that is intended to be studied at a desk. We often refer to the 'Gospel writers' as if they sat in a library and wanted their book to be studied in the way we want our books read; but this is the error of thinking they live in our modern world. The Gospels were composed to be encountered *aurally* – the ear listening to sounds – not by the eye scanning marks on a page. Moreover, they were to be heard in a group who heard them as their common narrative. So just as when, in our school days, we picked up a text of a play and read it, we were aware that reading *Hamlet* is not the same as seeing it, and seeing a film is not as good for understanding *Hamlet* as seeing a live play; so we must think of the Gospels as someone, the evangelists originally, giving a live recitation, and with the group listening. Picking up a Bible and reading a Gospel as if it were a report on Jesus' religious or ethical thoughts is just as alien to the author's expectations about his audience as reading *Macbeth* without at least imagining a stage and a packed auditorium.

Everyone knows the difference between an expert's handbook on how a computer works and *Computing for Dummies* – though they share the same form: the training manual. One assumes you already know a vast amount about the subject, the other that you know little and, indeed, might be sceptical about the whole area. The Gospels' composers assumed that those who would hear them already knew a great deal about Jesus, the background of the Old Covenant, the group's way of life, what was expected of them, and that they had already chosen baptism and were committed to the group, assembled regularly for their meal at which they blessed the Father for what he had done in Jesus, and now wanted to recall the life, teaching, death and resurrection of the one they followed as Lord. So when they heard the teaching of the sermon on the mount (Matt. 5—7) they had already learned much of it as simple instructions in the *Didache* and had accepted it. When they heard that Jesus rose and appeared among his disciples on a Sunday (John 20.1, 13, 19, 26) they already accepted this, for this was the very reason they were there listening to the evangelist as part of the group. The Gospels were written by believers for believers. They are 'insider' documents, not propaganda nor apologetics – indeed, we have to wait until the middle of the second century before we meet a text by a Christian that claims to be written for a non-Christian audience.

Practically, this awareness of audience has profound implications. For example, it means that we should not expect that someone who rejects belief in God or in Christianity would find the Gospels compelling – they were not written to satisfy the questions of such a person. Similarly, we have to think about how we imagine the Gospels' first audiences: do we think of a gathering of believers for a meal (an event that would later be formalized into the ritual of the Eucharist) listening to a performance, or do we think of a small group sitting around reading Bibles which rest on their knees and then discussing what it might mean? When Christians do gather at the Eucharist and listen to the Gospel proclaimed, are they listening or are they each reading along in books?

The question of audience is crucial: get it wrong – whether you are producing a television programme or encountering a Gospel – and the message will be lost or skewed.

Story

Every good biography, every narrative, has a storyline (although in modern academic books there is often a lot of conscious effort to hide this fact). The storyline is the perspective that draws one into the document, it is about emotional involvement, it is about identity. When someone says that they do not like X's book on a subject, but do like Y's book on the same subject, what has often made the difference is the story. In most secular narratives, the storyline takes the form of being written from one side or another: books from our side adopt a 'perspective', the other side's books have a 'bias'. Clearly, books about the Second World War will have a different story by someone from the Allies' side from that of someone from the Axis side. An American will be involved, and involve the readers, in a different way from someone from Britain writing about 1940, or a Jewish writer considering the destruction of the Warsaw Ghetto.

The composers of the Gospels assume that we are engaged emotionally with the Christ. He is neither a distant figure nor an interesting teacher for his audience, and so the story is that of how he loved his disciples, taught them and interacted with them: we are involved, and we appreciate more just who we are as Christians when we hear them. The hearer is not intended to be unmoved by the Passion accounts, nor expected to stick his hand up during one of Matthew's set-piece sermons and blurt out 'But that is not consistent with what you said on such and such an occasion when you then said . . .' The hearer is expected to be drawn into the story, to identify with Jesus as the Lord, the Anointed One, in just the same way we are drawn into a thrilling film, when, sitting on the edge of our seat, we are anxious for the heroes of the tale to escape before the time runs out, which we can hear ticking in the background.

This idea that the Gospels have a storyline is problematic for many people: we think that as soon as we detect a story, then the document is biased, compromised, useless. But the objectivity that such a rejection implies is wholly illusory: no one, not even someone from another planet, thinks or writes in such a way. Recall the last time you heard someone tell you of an inter-personal conflict in which she or he was involved. If that person is a relative or friend you will sympathize and accept; if you then hear from the other party you will be quick to point out that they have not got the story right; while a judge will invoke the legal principle of 'let the other side be heard'. The Gospels were composed by disciples for disciples, and they expect you to be drawn into deeper discipleship through recollection on the life, death and resurrection of Jesus; or, in more theological language: to encounter the Gospels is part of entering the Paschal Mystery.

History

In any narrative there are details of life that can be authenticated, content that can be verified, and details that are simply true or false. Since we cannot rerun time, the key test we always use is that of the detail being possible. So, did Jesus meet a woman at a well? The test is this: could Jesus have met people (yes), did he travel (yes), could women be seen at wells (yes), so the story in John 4.5–42 should not trouble us as to the plausibility of the meeting. However, 'history' is never met in a document outside of 'form' and 'audience'.

The biographer cannot relate everything (especially if the product is going to be presented orally: there is a natural limit to the length of a Gospel) and so selects; and an audience will soon tire if there are umpteen bits that seem to repeat one another. So the material will be put together, grouped, summarized, and given the variety of local colour. Moreover, notes of explanation, commentary and background will creep in, and some will then be expanded, while perhaps others get shortened – so the actual telling of the history is not a fixed element carved in stone. Tradition is dynamic as each evangelist sought to improve his tale as communication, and to adapt it to the understanding of his audience. So the sayings of Jesus that are found in what we call 'the sermon on the mount' are found in a very different order, with different emphases and contexts in Luke, and bits are found otherwise in Mark and John. So was there a sermon on the mount? Most probably not, but this is simply pointing out that the editorial work of this evangelist is the editorial work of this evangelist: it is not to suggest that he is a fraud. Anyone communicating a complex narrative must use poetic or historical licence – just as an historical film must – so that the large picture of the life and death of Jesus can be told without the multi-volume work that John hints at: 'But there are also many other things which Jesus did; were every one of them to be written, I suppose that the world itself could not contain the books that would be written' (John 21.25 RSV). Lastly, every culture has its own style of writing history – ours gives a premium to analysis over the repetition of details – and in the culture of the time, a good history was one that was 'orderly' (Luke 1.3) and where 'the style of the story delights the ears of those who read the work' (2 Macc. 15.39 NRSV). Therefore, we should expect that the evangelists have each put their own order on what may have come to them as a jumble of facts and sayings, and then they tried to make their narratives elegant as well.

Because we have to sift out the editorial work of each evangelist and note how details are altered in recollection and repetition, the work of establishing what we can say about 'the historical Jesus' is not an easy matter. While very few will ever learn the art of sifting historical details from historical narratives, and few will even read their books, it is enough to note that one cannot dismiss a detail (or a whole Gospel) because it is contradicted in another Gospel (and people have been attacking the Gospels in this way since the later second century); likewise, one cannot simply assert that a detail is factually correct just because it is not contradicted or because it is found in all four Gospels (e.g., it could be an early editorial hand, followed by the others).

Myth

No two questions are as often confused by those who encounter the Gospels as those concerned with history and myth. History is that which, of its nature, belongs to the normal world of our experience – it concerns what could happen to any human being up to the time of death and burial; myth is everything else we hear in the Gospels. This is what *does not belong* to the world of normal expectation: healings, exorcisms, appearances of angels, feedings of the multitude, voices from heaven, and above all the accounts of the resurrection, the appearances and the ascension. These are the parts of the Gospel that the evangelist expects us to treat as different and 'other'. We are to view them as uniquely related to the identity of Jesus which 'flesh and blood has not revealed . . . but my Father who is in heaven' (Matt. 16.17 RSV). We often try to explain away these parts as if they were just confused in memory by the early tradition (e.g., explain Jesus walking on the water as an illusion when he was on the shore – Mark 6.48), but these rationalizations ignore the basic fact: the evangelist wants you to recognize that this is not an event belonging to the world of history, but is wondrous, miraculous, non-normal. Moreover, if someone who does not believe that Jesus is the Lord says that she or he finds such and such a story nonsense, it is no use arguing with that person: you can argue about an historical fact (e.g., was Napoleon depressed in Moscow in 1812?), but not about an 'event' that claims as its basic quality to lie beyond the bounds of history (e.g., an angel appeared to Mary – Luke 1.26–38).

The question of audience is crucial: if you were listening to the evangelists when they were alive, you had already made your commitment to Jesus as Lord, and confessed that he had risen from the dead – despite *historical* claims to the contrary: Matthew 28.12–15. It is from this perspective of commitment that you now hear these mythic events, and rather than asking whether or not you think them likely (the correct response to historical details), you view them as 'windows' into the world that God has revealed, which is beyond our normal senses. Here the myths are expressed in terms we can imagine, but relate to 'events' we cannot encounter historically. Myths use the elements of finite creation that we can envisage so that we can glimpse *through* these accounts the world beyond our imagining. Trying to figure out these mythic elements as if they could make sense apart from the fundamental structures of discipleship is as vain as trying to fix a broken computer program with a hammer, a saw and a few nails. Equally, it is useless trying to insist to someone who is not a disciple that 'these things happened', for one cannot parallel them with historical experience; while with a disciple it is a waste of time wondering if 'they happened', for the task is to see what they reveal about God and his Christ. Faced with a miracle story, our challenge is to discover what it tells us about God who is greater than the creation and our imaginations.

Task

The last question is that of task, and it is usually the very first concern of the composer of a text: why compose this text in this way for this audience? The reason for some texts is very simple: the bill or invoice, for example, is composed to show what has been done and how much the recipient owes the sender. By contrast, it is very difficult to establish why someone has written a poem. Perhaps it is because the subject seemed too subtle for prose, perhaps because the poet rejoices in beautiful language, perhaps so that it can be put to music or easily remembered, or perhaps just for fun. Some books are written to communicate a body of facts and information (e.g. a car maintenance manual), some are intended to amuse us (e.g. a lot of novels), and others are written to persuade us that we should adopt an attitude or position on a topic (e.g. a political manifesto, an advert, or a report showing that smoking is dangerous).

The task of the Gospels seems so simple as not to require thinking: to tell us about Jesus, to persuade us to believe in him, or to give us the basic starting point of faith. However, when we think a little further – recall what we said about audience and myth – we see that it is actually a very profound question. The audience already knew a lot about Jesus, they already believed, and they belonged to a community that would show its members the way to live. So why did evangelists travel round the churches retelling their long, elegant tales? Part of the answer lies in the title they gave them: 'Gospels'. A Gospel was a particular type of good news: politically, it was the statement that the ruler had conquered his foes and that the city was now under that victor's protection. Declaring the 'good news' was akin to a victory celebration and identified those taking part with the victor. In the case of Christians, the good news was the Lord had conquered and his people – those listening – were safe under his protection, liberation and love. Moreover, the act of gathering and hearing the Gospel proclaimed was not simply a study session or a performance, but was one of the ways that the risen Lord was present. Just as the account went beyond history and revealed mythically the inner identity of Jesus, so retelling the story was not simple recollection but encounter. To gather in his name and recall him was to have him present in their midst (Matt. 18.20).

We have texts from the early churches whose task was training (the *Didache*), correction (Paul's letters to the Corinthians; the letter of Jude), formal instruction (Paul to the Romans), to establish links between all the churches (Acts), and to offer encouragement (1 Peter), but in the Gospels we have the task of offering in the recitation a means of encountering the Christ and embracing his act of liberation, deliverance and redemption. It is this task of the Gospels that made them valued in a special way from the later first century onwards and why they have, since their composition, figured in the weekly meal gatherings of the churches.

Using six questions to approach 'what is a Gospel?' may seem to be a complex way of tackling one question, but it does have the advantage of generating significant answers to many queries that crop up as we listen to these core Christian texts today.

3

A 'people of the book' or the books of a people?

In recent years the phrase 'the people of the book' has become part of our religious vocabulary, and been widely adopted without apparent difficulty. Of Islamic origin – denoting those religions that were not simply 'pagan' – it has become a phrase whose value lies in its inclusiveness. It seems to embrace the three Abrahamic faiths – the great monotheistic religions – and respect their traditions, their sacred book or books. It even includes, in Westerners' usage, Islam, the one religion not included in its original formulation. However, leaving aside the desire for terms with universal embrace, is it, *as a self-description*, free of problems?

First thoughts say that 'a people of the book' is a fine description of us: the evidence abounds. We are so familiar with the notion of 'the Bible' – or should that be 'The Bible' – that any essential book can be referred to as 'the bible of . . .' It would appear that all you want to know about Christianity is in it, and there is a long tradition of assuming that preaching Christianity is 'preaching the Bible' or making the Bible available. If you have the book, then you can get the religion. So making Bibles available in hotel rooms, in foreign languages, in cheap editions, at every turn is seen as a good activity in itself. 'Go therefore and make disciples of all nations' (Matt. 28.19 NRSV) becomes in practice the need to provide a book and reading skills. So who are these Christians, who is this people (if they have such a trans-individual identity)? Those who read and value this book, 'the Bible'.

Turning to Christianity's origins – the life of Jesus (whom we confess as the Father's 'christ' – the one he has anointed) and his followers (some of whose writings we read in 'the Book') – may lessen our confidence in the description. In turn, problems with it may prompt us to examine our attitudes to that book's place in Christianity and wonder what price we pay for so widespread a misunderstanding.

35

There is only one reference in early Christian literature to Jesus writing: on the ground with his finger (John 8.8). This is unusual for a religious leader: we have no book by, or attributed to, our founder. For someone founding a religion of the book, this is surely an oversight. We have early books about him, the Gospels, but they explicitly claim to be *about* him, not by him. When later Christians attributed letters to Jesus, these never attracted more than peripheral curiosity, and never achieved the status of being heard in liturgical assemblies – which was the key factor in determining which texts were held to be authoritative and which not.

The gospel of Jesus lies in the notion of the kingdom: the future God wants for us – a community not a set of individuals – is one where each member is loved by God, invited into a relationship with God, and started on a journey towards a heavenly banquet. The end is coming, but the distinctive vision was that this was the great ingathering of the kingdom, rather than the great crunch – a message that characterized other preachers of the day, notably John the Baptist, and that remained within Christian tradition through his followers retaining their views of the future while accepting that Jesus was the Christ. Community, being formed now and eventually becoming the kingdom, and so a different view of the present and the future, lay at the centre of his work; and it seems that it was in living that community that his disciples discovered the nature of his message. Only when you live in a Christian community can you discover the Christian message: the message is a function of community, not vice versa. The book is not the message, but a practical ancillary to the message, and that follows on joining the community.

This sequence continues among his followers: before we have any writings, we have churches – actual small communities who are gathering, offering thanks to the Father in Jesus' name in their common meal, and so proclaiming the Lord's death until he comes (1 Cor. 11.23–26). These communities sought to initiate new members into their relationship with God – they saw themselves as the inheritors of the covenant, and the new Israel, the new people of God: they were a community who knew the way of life, gathered, celebrated and hoped together (the *Didache* is our best guide to practice). And it was these communities that retold the story of Jesus and welcomed the travellers who could tell that story, not in fragments as most people do, but from beginning to end: evangelists. These travelling announcers left 'recordings' of their story of Jesus, and they were heard and reheard in the gatherings of the community. We think of a book as an object of reading where each of us is the reader; an ancient book was a way of hearing someone not physically present: it was for hearing. It is better to think of our Gospels by analogy with tapes or CDs of a performance in a group, than by thinking of them as equivalents of a modern book intended for study. The ideal recipient of a Gospel was someone who could listen; the ideal recipient of a modern book is someone who can read. We see this tension between now and then at every act of worship: ancient texts are read aloud, yet most people feel they would understand it better if they were to read it for themselves – listening just does not seem enough! The book's message seems more real, more important, than the action of a part of a community listening together. This attitude is an oft-forgotten chasm between us and the authors of our sacred books.

Recalling that books were a function of community gatherings, indeed meal gatherings, we can appreciate why consistency between Gospel stories was not a priority, nor did they generate the fascination with Gospel-discrepancies that drives much exegetical concern by Christians and equally vehement exploitation by those wanting to attack Christianity. Each evangelist sought to tell a story that was larger than history, sought to capture mystery in his account, and it was played and replayed because in the act of remembering by the community, they encountered the mystery of Jesus as the Christ who established their community and communion. They were not consulting the biography of their ideologue. Interestingly, it was the second-century opponents of Christianity, e.g. Celsus, who first imagined those valued memories as equivalent to a philosopher's book or a religion's manifesto. The community was united by its relationship, its covenant – *testamentum* in Latin – with the Lord, not by its common ideology or its book. This new covenant was founded upon an older covenant with the first People of God – *israel* in Hebrew – and so they told and retold the story of that relationship. In this recitation they privileged those documents which were held to be original (so they took over Scriptures in the form of the Judaism of the Hellenistic world: the Septuagint form of what was for them the books of the Old Covenant) and authentic (the writings of apostles or of evangelists heard in all the communities). It would be a mixture of lazy thinking, sloppy theology, and a much later attitude to reading and books that would turn the phrases 'the old testament' and 'the new testament' into the titles of anthologies, and then see any relationship, covenant or *testamentum* as resulting from the book, rather than the reverse. In the process, the book was made into the mega-sacrament revealing God – an attitude we see in the way we use the book as an object in swearing an oath (compare Matt. 5.34 and Jas. 5.12 for an earlier attitude) – forgetting that it was Jesus who is *the* sacrament, whose presence is manifested in and by the community – which, in turn, preserved its memories as formed by its teachers in its repeated listening which, in turn, needed writings.

This interchange of book with community and communion took place over centuries and now is so embedded that it is probably beyond being rectified – witness the number who cannot countenance any criticism of the book's perfection or all-sufficiency. Moreover, our culture is happier, first, with the idea of religion as a personal ideology than a community's relationship, and, second, with the idea of having a set book we can browse individually, than with a memory needing community interpretation. Yet anyone who preaches in continuity with the earliest Christians cannot be happy with the situation where the book supplants the Spirit who animates the community. In the face of our cultural inheritance, railing against the past generates more heat than light, but we should be careful about incidentally reinforcing confused ideas by appealing to faulty analogies.

It is worthwhile considering the following:

- The Bible connotes the notion of a sacred book, a single coherent entity, sacral in some way in itself. Consider the usage of the Gospels: 'the scriptures' (e.g. Luke 24.45). It supposes a plurality, a diversity, a collection that functions within the wider context of the community whose writings they are.
- We sometimes point to the Scriptures as a metaphor of the teaching – whether it is part of a formal ordination ceremony or an evangelical preacher holding the book as an informal symbol of authority; but this implies that the collection is a manifesto. Here is what we hold: complete and entire! But our 'holding' is always incomplete, always flawed, always deformed in the selfishness of our own lives. The task is to be able to hear the clash between our memories

and our hopes, rather than to 'download' what can be put between two covers.

- For many, religion's task is to give ritual sanction to a code of acceptable behaviour: the Bible is a law code. Preachers, tasked with introducing a person, Jesus, collude and cite the book as if it were an expression of legislation. Such appeals make for forceful preaching but ignore the role of societies in the production of law codes as well as their role in producing scriptures. Treating our Scriptures as a law code ignores why and how they became our Scriptures in the first place. The phrase 'the law of God' loses much of its offence when more carefully defined as 'this is how an earlier community understood the demands of obedience to a God-focused life': accuracy in preaching is, in the long term, to be preferred to punchlines.
- Lastly, the books of the people should not be construed as if they ever could contain the mystery of God: God is always greater than our greatest imaginings.

Part 2

LECTIONARIES

4

Is a lectionary a good idea?

Until very recently only people involved in the planning of worship ever used the word 'lectionary' and there was no specific book you could pick up in your hands with the word 'Lectionary' written on its cover; most churches did actually use them, but located the contents of their lectionaries inside other books (> Appendix 6). Thus Catholics had the readings printed in their missal, while Anglicans had the readings for Sundays printed in their Book of Common Prayer while other readings were printed as lists of references in 'The Calendar, with the Table of Lessons' printed at the front of the book. So a lectionary is first and foremost *the plan and arrangement of readings from Scriptures over a given period*. However, there are other events in a church's life that occur from time to time – some common (e.g. baptisms and marriages), others very rare (e.g. opening a new church building) – for which selections of readings are needed, and so these too need to be catered for by the Lectionary's plan.

So if at its simplest a lectionary is a list of passages, human nature dictates that it will not long remain so: the effort of marking a Bible (and remember that until the thirteenth century it was extremely rare to have an entire collection of the Scriptures between two covers: in most cases it needed a shelf with between five and seven volumes) over and over again meant that sooner rather than later someone would extract all the pieces and arrange them together in the order in which they were going to appear in worship. The first reference to such a specific collection comes from Marseille around 460, and quite soon after that we find that liturgical books with the various prayers for the president also contain the readings to be used on that occasion (> Palazzo 1998, 83–105). This began a practice of putting readings and all the other prayers between two covers – just as we find it in the Tridentine Missal and the Book of Common Prayer – which lasted until very recently. Moreover, so long as the readings at the Eucharist consisted of just a single annual sequence of an epistle and a Gospel – and the Anglican Lectionary in the Book of

43

Common Prayer was virtually identical with that found in the Tridentine Missal[1] – it made sense both in terms of convenience and cost to print everything in one book. So why now has the Lectionary emerged as a separate large book on its own?

When the annual pattern of readings was examined in the mid twentieth century as part of the reform of the liturgy being carried out by many churches, it was found to be seriously deficient both in its plan (it had arisen by a series of accidents and so while it could be laid out as a 'plan' it was not planned) and in the limited exposure it gave to the Gospels (and consequently other parts of the Scriptures) in the central act of worship (> Bugnini 1990, 416; and Hageman 1982). Among Catholics this process – spurred on by the Second Vatican Council – led to an almost completely new Lectionary being published in 1969 which not only increased massively the quantity of Scripture used, but also laid it out in a careful plan that tried – we will discuss the compromises in detail further on – to pay close attention to the nature of the Gospels as they were used in the first churches (> Chapter 5). This Lectionary was published as a list, but when it was put into actual use it became a large book (the first English edition had 1,037 large two-column pages) distinct from the book containing the prayers for the Eucharist, and so the modern 'lectionary' (a physical object, a book) came into being. As other churches sought to incorporate the insights of the liturgical movement (> Fenwick and Spinks 1995) into their worship there was widespread admiration for the new Roman arrangement and it was widely followed in its general arrangement, but with each church seeking to accommodate some specific needs of their own, and tweaking it to try to improve it here and there. Moreover, since every lectionary is the product of necessary compromises, each committee approached one or more of these choices with slightly differing emphases. This resulted in a lectionary produced in America known as the *Revised Common Lectionary (RCL)* in 1992 (> Bower 1996; and West 1997).

---

[1] The major difference is that the BCP was one week behind the Tridentine Missal because while the Catholics counted 'Sundays after Pentecost', the Anglicans counted 'Sundays after Trinity' – therefore, for example, we find the exact same readings set out for Catholics on the 'third Sunday after Pentecost' as those which the Anglicans would hear one week later on the 'third Sunday after Trinity' (> Appendix 6).

RCL was authorized for use in the Church of England in 1996; and then some further tweaking (there is no such thing as a perfect lectionary – there is always room for adjustments) resulted in the *Common Worship Lectionary* of 1999. The details of the relationships of these three Lectionaries (*RL, RCL, CWL*) – which together form a single lectionary family – can be followed in detail in Appendices 1–5, but the relationship can be summarized in this way:

- since the Gospel reading forms the core of all three Lectionaries they are substantially the same – and the rationale underpinning *RL* is adopted in its entirety (> Chapter 5);
- in the use of the Old Testament *RCL* departs from *RL*, and this is followed as an option by *CWL*;
- in the use of the New Testament (apart from the Gospels) *RCL* modifies *RL*, and *RCL* is followed by *CWL*;
- *RCL* tweaks details of *RL* and in these cases is invariably followed by *CWL*;
- where *RCL* differs from *RL*, *CWL* often keeps both choices, offering them as alternatives.

However, because they form a single lectionary family they are best studied together, for this not only explains their common arrangements of readings, but comparison allows us to note how different emphases animated those selecting the readings and lets us examine the various solutions used when confronted with the problem of presenting meaningful snippets from larger texts which are usually very alien in culture to that of modern congregations.

The fact that many Christian churches – often only noted for their embargoes on one another in matters relating to the Eucharist – are all sharing what is, in effect, a single Lectionary should be a matter of ecumenical rejoicing and should allow for a greater sharing of resources in preparing ministers and people for sharing the Word of God. As the late Kenneth Stevenson wrote in the introduction to the *CWL*: 'the fruit of ecumenical collaboration, biblical as well as liturgical, it can claim to be a significant landmark in the Church catholic's attention to what the Spirit has to say to us as we gather around the Lord's Table.'[2]

---

[2] *CWL*, p. viii.

But after nearly two decades of use, there is little to show from this remarkable convergence of often very different views of Scripture. Indeed, while texts of prayers have caused endless faction-fighting within communions, and there have been very public discussions about which translation to use (Anglicans arguing over which Bible version, Catholics over whether prayers should sound Latinate or not), there has been little or no discussion about the Lectionary! What discussion has taken place has been on the most mundane level – Catholics wanting to know if they can 'drop' difficult texts, Anglicans wanting further 'alternative' texts – which in each case eats away at the Lectionary's overall structure, thereby undermining its fundamental rationale. The fact that these demands have been accommodated, more or less, in both churches shows that all those involved have a relatively weak grasp of the structure of the Lectionary and its key aims as a tool for expounding the Gospels in course of the liturgy.

The pros and cons of lectionaries

The major argument against lectionaries is the claim that they stifle the freedom of the community to select the readings that are most appropriate to them, in their situation, in their moment. This objection invokes many of the favourite themes of our society: relevance, sensitivity to the locality and the moment, and freedom of choice. However, the arguments against this level of choice are overwhelming:

- It will not be the community's choice, but the choice of the minister or of an articulate and/or assertive sub-group who will impose their choice. In one place, that might be driven by the 'desire to communicate' and so readings would be chosen which are 'easy for children to understand' (how many ancient adult theological texts are that simple?) or 'to assert the Gospel's values' and so the readings might well dwell on sin, judgement and apocalyptic themes (just note how a few texts keep coming up on religious television).
- Every reader of the Scriptures has a group of texts that speak to her or him, and everyone tends to arrange other texts around their favourite or key texts. Those who read or study the Scriptures

regularly have books or passages they like and books or passages they prefer to avoid: can you list yours? Each of us (and each church) has, often unconsciously, a canon within the canon. So if choice is left to us, some texts would be heard many times over, others hardly at all.

- The books of the Scriptures have an integrity of their own. Mark preached a gospel with a definite aim, and so too did Matthew, and so too did Luke – and Matthew and Luke, separately, clearly wanted to depart from Mark; while John wanted to take a different tack altogether. It is the sum total of these different perspectives that make up our memory – quarrying them for the bits that we like is disrespectful of the tradition by which the faith has reached us, and converts the Gospels into consumable commodities.

- We all crave that which speaks to us, which resonates in our lives, which meets our needs. But this not only puts me or us at the centre of the universe – an ironic position to be in when we have gathered to worship the Creator – but ignores the first call of the gospel: 'The time is fulfilled, and the kingdom of God has come near; repent, and believe in the good news' (Mark 1.15 NRSV). The 'good news' is often that which does not speak comfort to us but sets before us the challenge of discipleship. Self-selection tends either to be comforting of the status quo or else its polar opposite: someone who thinks that the 'good news' equates to making people feel uncomfortable.

- Whenever a group decides to 'select the readings' for any celebration (other than for a one-off event), they eventually start arguing about choices so that what should be a moment of common listening to a commonly possessed text becomes a time of friction and divisiveness.

- Given the sheer size of our Scriptures – and the sheer size of the individual parts (e.g. Gospels, letters, prophets, other books) – if we are to have anything like a representative coverage one has to make decisions not just for a day or a month or even a season – but over a minimum of a year: such a level of planning requires much time, resources and research, and is, in effect, beyond what any ordinary congregation could reasonably accomplish.

- Whenever someone has a sermon they want to preach and then goes hunting for suitable readings to go with it, the Scriptures have been reduced to the role of 'supporting cast' to our own ideas;

yet those same people often appeal to the Scriptures – for example by holding a Bible in the their hands as they speak – as the basis of their authority to preach.

That said, there will be times when a sudden event (e.g. the death of a world leader) will be on everyone's lips as they gather, or when everyone will be talking about some other common concern at the time (e.g. the World Cup final being played that evening) when it would be silly to celebrate the liturgy as if these events were not happening. On these occasions, common sense should rule: no liturgy can remain alive and slavishly follow a book. But remember the other side of the coin: Catholics have used this Lectionary for about forty years and have already made so many formally approved 'exceptions' that in some communities, where each exception is followed, the whole plan of the Lectionary has been obscured, if not positively ignored. The same phenomenon already affects those using *RCL* and *CWL* (note the number of additional special cases added by *CWL* to *RCL*), and with every passing year the temptations to cater for the 'immediate' or to have a 'special theme' for a particular Sunday in contrast to an ordered pattern of readings will increase.

The other most common objection to the Lectionaries comes from those who hold that one must respect the biblical texts that one reads, and consequently read them in 'their natural units'; and that anything other than that is a case of imposing an editorial slant by means of a pair of scissors. This objection to lectionaries is far more serious than that based on limiting a community's freedom, because it is true that any act of selecting will inevitably omit, any manner of arranging will inevitably slant the way that a text is read, and every combination of readings in a particular liturgy will affect how each passage is heard and appreciated. However, if we consider the alternatives to running these risks, we see the need for compromise:

- Just look at the size of what is available for reading! Does one read everything? Then how long have people to be there? If one were to read a whole Gospel – a very well-defined unit – it would take a minimum of three hours. Paul's longer letters take not much less. The nature of human beings means that we have to break the texts up and use them in chunks – the task is to pick the right-sized portions and arrange them well.

- Just what attention span can one expect from people? Some people can listen to a great deal of Scripture (or any other text), follow it, and take it in. But bear in mind that most of the books in our Scriptures do not employ the kind of logical arrangement we expect from modern books or lectures. Following a long sequence of oracles in a prophet, a series of laws in Numbers or Leviticus, or a series of sayings in a Gospel can be pretty tough work even for those familiar with the texts. Then recall that the average person's attention span is far shorter than that of those who opt to specialize in theological studies. While most preachers are happy to think in terms of a ten-minute attention span (for their homilies), most people in the communications business think of three minutes as a large quantity of time (> Kwok 2010)! Sometimes there is a pious rejoinder in this form: people are more attentive when listening to the Word of God. This is undoubtedly true for some, but a quick test is to ask people immediately after the Eucharist to recall two of the readings. It is a sobering experiment if carried out on an ordinary congregation on an ordinary Sunday.

- The readings are not part of a course intended to be an introduction to the study of the Bible. The way we hear the Scriptures, in worship, as a community is very different from the way we attend to them in study. Both approaches are complementary: without study their wealth is not only hidden but their message and significance can be easily abused; without an appreciation of their role in worship, their study can become simply an examination of texts from an ancient culture. But, equally, worship and study should not be confused. In liturgy, the act of recollection is intended to enrich our memories so that we, in our collective imagination, enter into a moment of familiarity with God. In study, we seek to answer our questions about that which we believe, search out our past, and by a process of examination discover more about the implications of faith. Teaching and proclamation are related, but distinct activities – and should not be fused into one.

- If we try to take in too much at any one time, or take in too many diverse messages – which can easily happen (e.g. the different topics of the second reading in contrast to the Gospel, or in *RCL* (and optionally in *CWL*) when one can have an Old Testament reading, a letter and a Gospel without connection), then what usually happens is that we take in next to nothing.

- It should be kept in mind that the seating arrangements, the general ambience, and the various subsections of any average congregation (e.g. children alongside adults, some who know a great deal sitting beside those who know little, 'seekers' with those who have been Christians from childhood) do not make the Sunday liturgy an ideal situation for the sort of deep immersion in the Scriptures desired by those in favour of extended readings. By contrast, there are many who, from the experience of the present Lectionary, consider that it tries to present too much.

One other stream of argument against lectionaries, or more precisely preaching based on a lectionary, comes from those who think of the assembly as a forum for imparting church teaching or moral exhortation. For this group either the sermons should be 'instructional' following some plan – expounding 'the articles' of the creed is a favourite – or perhaps even the readings should be selected around this doctrinal spine. This notion is perverse for several reasons. First, the primary proclamation of the Church is the gospel of Jesus the Christ which is encountered in the accounts of the four evangelists (> Stanton 2004); all doctrinal schemata are attempts to formulate that in a manner suitable for the classroom – but such doctrinal formulae cannot replace the gospel and the Gospels. Second, it confuses the catechetical gathering with the actual celebration of our life in Christ. Third, it fails to recognize that the purpose of proclamation – followed by a homily – in the community assembled is an encounter with the risen Christ, not the imparting of knowledge nor the promulgation of a morality (> Sloyan 1987). While 'the sermon' is a form of religious address, a special kind of lecture, a 'homily' is a liturgical act: an exploration of a heard passage of Scripture whose aim is to help the gathering to encounter the mystery being celebrated.

However, the most important point in favour of the present Lectionary is that, outside of the seasons of Advent-Christmas and Lent-Easter when readings are focused on these events, it provides an outline, one per year, of the teaching of Matthew, Mark and Luke, thus allowing their three distinct views of what it means to believe in Jesus and differing ways of remembering him – what are, in effect, their three Christologies – to be heard. Not only does this provide as rich a feast of Gospel texts as probably can be managed, but presents an opportunity to the preachers to explore in homilies a very wide variety of approaches to the mystery of Christ.

Compromises

Compromise is inevitable in lectionary design: there is no 'perfect' lectionary, and when we examine the nature of the compromises it becomes clear that there cannot be a perfect lectionary as every lectionary involves making choices. However, not all lectionaries are equal. Most lectionaries in the history of Christianity have been the result of some bits of obvious planning (e.g., they have one of the nativity stories for Christmas, and Acts 2.1–11 for Pentecost), some bits to 'fill in the gaps' often with a nod in the direction of 'continuous reading' (i.e., a series of readings which follow one another from the same biblical book) and a string of historical blunders that have been codified (indeed made sacrosanct) through long use. The Lectionary more or less common to the Tridentine Missal and the BCP is a good example of such 'partial planning' combined with muddle (> Appendix 6). Thus, the modern Lectionary is exceptional in that the planners openly acknowledged the compromises that had to be made and deliberately sought to find the best solution. Everyone using the Lectionary could argue that his or her solution to one or other of the problems posed is better than what is in the printed text, yet, overall, the planners have achieved a remarkable cover and balance. The compromises fall, roughly, under these headings:

Size

There is just so much biblical material available that much, if not most, has to be omitted. Put another way, there are always far more good claims for some text to be included than there are available slots. Virtually all lectionaries in Christian history have tried to cope with this on the basis of a one-year cycle which has the benefits of simplicity, economy of resources and repetition. The present Lectionary sacrifices these benefits by opting for a three-year Sunday cycle[3] which

---

[3] There is a complementary, but independent, two-year weekday cycle, but since that does not affect the Sunday Lectionary, it can be ignored here.

allows for almost three times as many passages to be chosen. Some wanted, or still want, a four-year cycle, but there the compromise in favour of simplicity and against repetition won the day.[4]

Concentration

Related to the issue of size is the question of where one concentrates one's focus given that the Scriptures are not a homogeneous mass, but made up of two testaments each with divisions within them. Does one try to give equal exposure to everything: Old Testament and New Testament, then law, prophets, history, wisdom, apocalyptic, Gospels (and between individual Gospels), Paul's letters, others' letters, history, apocalyptic? There is a certain logic to such general exposure to the tradition – it is the rationale behind many 'Bible survey modules' in theological training and of many books which take 'seeing the Bible whole' as their agenda. However, the danger with such survey approaches is that they can end up as 'a bit of everything and nothing much of anything', so the Lectionary makers opted for a concentration on the Gospels. This decision was primary in their eyes because of how they conceived the purpose of a lectionary for use at celebrations of the Eucharist. The whole event is a celebration of the gathering's identity in Christ and of his presence in the midst of the gathering (Matt. 18.20),[5] and so the recollection of his presence in the Gospels – an action first explicitly described by Justin in the mid second century – had to have, in their view, pre-eminence. So *the core of the Lectionary's architecture is to be found in its selection of Gospels* – and for RL the use of the Old Testament is regulated by that choice. That said, in the Lectionary there is also an unrelated selection (during ordinary times of the year) of New Testament letters so that they will get a hearing. Meanwhile,

---

[4] For an account of these discussions and compromises, > Bugnini 1990, 406–25.

[5] It is worth noting that the Roman Catholic Church radically expanded its formal theology of the presence of the Christ in the liturgy in the aftermath of Vatican II (> Flannery 1975, 4–5 [*Sacrosanctum Concilium* 7]). The *Instruction on the Roman Missal* conceived of four presences of the Christ: amidst the assembled people, the word, the minister, and the sacramental species (1969 edn, n. 7 / 2002 edn, n. 27). However, while this may seem jejune in terms of evolution of the notion of sacramental presence over the past four decades, it is still a notion that has hardly impacted in the average Catholic parish.

the compilers of *RCL* opted for a distinct Old Testament sequence for most of the Sundays of Ordinary Time in order that that many of the great Old Testament stories could get a hearing as stories. In both cases, the decision was made on the basis of the importance of the Old Testament stories and New Testament letters in our Christian memory. For *RL* the route into the Old Testament was to link passages to each Gospel; *RCL* took the other side of the argument: knowing the great story would provide the framework for hearing the Gospel – hence it modified its selection strategy for a period of roughly six months each year (> Appendix 5). This is the background to the choice offered in *CWL* between 'continuous Old Testament readings' (following *RCL*) and 'related Old Testament readings' (following, with minor adjustments, *RL*). Compromise is not a dirty word, but a necessary principle, in the creation of a lectionary![6]

Times and texts

The liturgy is not simply a dull even noise in the background of the lives of Christians, nor is it like a metronome simply swinging in parallel with the passing of time. Time is more like a piece of music: it has its highs and lows, its stressed and unstressed moments, its feasts and its fasts, and then time which is just downright ordinary (> Bradshaw and Johnson 2011). So within the week there is the special stressed day of celebration, Sunday, and the rest of the week; and while all Sundays are equal, some Sundays 'are more equal than others': obviously Easter Day, but also the Sundays either side of Christmas and Easter. Indeed, one has to be pretty insensitive to how humans like festive time – and it seems to be a fundamental element in human experience (> Chilton 2002) – not to appreciate that Christmastime is not the same as a dull week in March or October!

It is this fact of Christian worship, that not every day is the same, that creates the greatest tension for lectionary makers. The problem arises from the fact that the texts we read were, for the most part, written to be heard as narratives – and, therefore, it having already been decided that they cannot be read in their entirety in a single session, the best way to hear them is through continuous reading: each day taking up the text where it was left off at the previous

---

[6] For an account of some of these discussions and compromises, > Hageman 1982.

gathering. But if you intend to celebrate a calendar of festivals, then you have to read Matthew 2.1–12 on the feast of the Epiphany. But if Matthew had a perspective, distinctive to him, of the good news – that too must be respected and needs to be heard. A lectionary based on feasts and seasons is known as an 'eclogadic lectionary', while one based on whole texts (distributed over a number of days) is called a 'continuous reading lectionary' – and the com-promises achieved in *RL*, *RCL* and *CWL* between these two forms of lectionary are perhaps the most ingenious element in modern Lectionary development.

Themes

However, before looking at how the Lectionary combined the feasts and seasons with continuous reading, we need to note one last com-promise: *themes*. A constant question posed of the Lectionary is 'why is it not built around themes?' The problem that this question exposes is what and who should choose the themes: any such selec-tion runs the risk of being an arbitrary imposition of a particular view of Christianity with its inevitable attendant slants and assump-tions. The notion of themes – usually embraced on the basis of its convenience as a teaching plan – would then expose the liturgy to the sort of individualism that the whole notion of lectionaries seeks to counter, while at the same time falling into the trap of subsuming the ministry of the word – which is part of a liturgy – within a classroom or lecture perspective. That said, there are 'days with themes' in the liturgy (e.g. Bible Sunday among Anglicans, Mission Sunday among Catholics) and days where themes are mixed up with seasons (e.g. the feast of the Holy Family among Catholics, Harvest Thanks-giving among Anglicans) and so the Lectionary has to make com-promises to fit in these celebrations. However, as a general rule, the more that 'special days' are allowed to displace the Lectionary's overall plan – and after forty years the Catholic Church has now collected nearly a dozen such days – the weaker the Lectionary appears. Indeed, the willingness of Catholic bishops' conferences to allow the Lectionary to be set aside so frequently suggests that, first, the Lectionary is still very poorly understood among Catholics, and, second, the high appreciation of the Scriptures inherent in the Lectionary's architecture has not developed to the extent that Vatican II hoped it would when it mandated the creation of the Lectionary.

However, for most people it is not a case of trying to decide whether or not they like having a lectionary, much less whether they would change it to one of their own devising – the Lectionary is simply there as a fact. That's what we do, and we do it week in and week out! The task is not to change it, but to appreciate it.

5

The present Lectionary: structures and arrangement

Historically lectionaries have been created in two ways. The first, and simplest, way is to opt for continuous reading (*lectio continua*) of texts because this allows biblical books to be appreciated whole, and it avoids any tendency to skip over 'unpleasant' bits. Pick a day as starting point, and then begin reading either a Gospel, a book of the Old Testament or an epistle, and keep going, day after day, or Sunday after Sunday, until the book is finished. Then start on another. Given that the Gospels – and these will always be the driving force in the readings for our gatherings for the Eucharist – are episodic in structure, this method is ideally suited to appreciating them: read one story or incident today, then move to the next tomorrow or next Sunday. Such lectionaries are known as 'continuous reading lectionaries'.

However, given that the liturgical year (> Bradshaw and Johnson 2011) is fundamental to Christian liturgy – a component of practice already established by the time the Acts of the Apostles was written – the method of continuous reading can never hold unrivalled sway. How could one read a parable text on Easter Day just because it was the next reading in a sequence? The very fact that the rudiments of the liturgical year may predate the Gospels we possess has meant that the nature of the day – for example, if it is the day of Pentecost – determines that the reading should be linked to the feast. So at Christmas we need to hear of Bethlehem; at Easter of the resurrection; and on 6 August of the Transfiguration.

The creators of the Lectionary therefore opted to have an eclogadic lectionary for the seasons, and a continuous reading lectionary for the rest of the year: the time often referred to in English, very aptly, as 'ordinary time'.[1] So we can think of the Lectionary as made

---

[1] In *RL* 'Ordinary Time' is used as an official designation in English for the Sundays outside of Advent-Christmas and Lent-Easter. The term was then adopted by *RCL*; and it is used in 'The Reader's Guide' to *CWL* (x and xi), but it is not used

up of three major parts paralleling the three periods of the year (see Table 5.1).

Table 5.1 The three major parts of the Lectionary

1	Advent	
	Christmas Day	Season determines readings.
	Christmastide	
3a	**Ordinary Time**	Semi-continuous reading of (1) Gospels with related Old Testament texts; (2) New Testament letters. There is no common theme between (1) and (2).
2	Lent	
	Easter Day	Season determines readings.
	Eastertide	
3b	**Ordinary Time**	*RL*: Semi-continuous reading of (1) Gospels with related Old Testament texts; (2) New Testament letters. There is no common theme between (1) and (2). *RCL*: Semi-continuous reading of (1) Gospels; (2) Old Testament narratives; (3) New Testament letters. There is no common theme between (1), (2) and (3). *CWL* allows a choice between reading strategies.

However, since the Lectionary is spread over a three-year cycle, there is a predominance of one of the first three evangelists (Matthew, Mark, Luke) in each of the years. So we can refer to the three years – with reference to the Gospels – as shown in Table 5.2.

Table 5.2 The three years and their Gospels

Year A	'The year of Matthew'
Year B	'The year of Mark'
Year C	'The year of Luke'

in the body of the book where the more cumbersome formulae of 'Sundays before', 'Sundays after' and 'Proper' have been used. On the notion of 'ordinary time' > O'Loughlin 2007, 34–6.

So how do we know which year of the Lectionary we are in? Which Gospel is read on Sundays in any calendar year is determined by the simple method of dividing the date by three: if the remainder is 1, then it is the first year of the cycle and the year of Matthew; if the remainder is 2, then it is the second year and the year of Mark; and, if the date is perfectly divisible, it is year 3, the year of Luke. So, for example:

2012 ÷ 3 = 670 'and two over', hence it is 'year 2'.
2016 ÷ 3 = 672 'and nothing over', hence it is 'year 3'.
2023 ÷ 3 = 674 'and one over', hence it is 'year 1'.

There is no need for a feat of memory or a special table: just a quick bit of division. From an ecumenical perspective this was an inspired way of determining the cycle when *RL* was produced because there is no 'Vatican-inspired Year Zero' telling people that a particular year is Year A – it is simply a matter of AD and maths!

Different evangelists – different perspectives on Jesus

To appreciate the Lectionary we must note that once the option of continuous reading of the Gospels in Ordinary Time was taken, there were still many other decisions as to what would and would not be included. There were three key factors facing the selectors: first, even in Mark – once the chapters after 11.1, relating to the final week in Jerusalem, are omitted since they are used in Lent and Holy Week – there is still too much material to distribute over the available number of Sundays unless very large sections (often made up of several stories) were read each Sunday; second, there are passages in 'the triple tradition' (where Matthew and Luke are reformulating material in Mark) so alike each other that they would be given undue prominence if read from each Gospel (and therefore, de facto, read each year), and so these had to be curtailed; and, third, there are parts of each Gospel text that for a variety of reasons are so problematic (e.g. corrupt texts, duplications, interpolations) that they are best omitted from public reading or pruned of erratic verses.[2] Hence the selectors describe their

---

[2] There is always a group who believe that one should 'take it as it comes' and not make such decisions, but this fails to take account of the jumble and muddle of history as these texts were transmitted down the centuries to us. For an introduction to the problems > Parker 2008.

work in the 1981 edition of *RL* not as 'continuous reading' but more precisely as 'semi-continuous'.

If we take the Gospel of Mark as an example, we have 'semi-continuous reading' up to the time Jesus arrives in Jerusalem and then some snippets from the Jerusalem discourses. The result was that the selectors had a total of 405 verses from between Mark 1.1 and 10.52 available to them for Ordinary Time. However, they used only about 190 of these (i.e., just under half the text), plus 20 verses from Mark 12—13, and 70 verses from John's Gospel. This selection was not just a case of pruning and dividing out what was left: knowing that they had to select, they deliberately adopted a policy of presenting the pieces of the Gospel as part of the larger plan to show the Gospel writers' intentions. They assumed that each of the Synoptics (the Gospels of Matthew, Mark and Luke) 'presents us with a recognisable' and, we might add, distinctive 'portrait of Christ and a *particular approach* [their italics] to his teaching'.[3] Their aim in this process of selection was outlined as 'allowing the main lines of the structure and theology of each . . . to be grasped by preacher and reader [which] should allow the message of each . . . to penetrate gradually into the consciousness of the faithful'. They then provided the three schemata they envisaged acting as the scaffolding over each year. But then, possibly recognizing that neither is what a text's audience hears static over time or cultures, nor does biblical scholarship stand still, they added that 'such schemes are not definitive, but it is hoped that they will be a help'. Each scheme will be examined in detail later in this chapter.

We get a flavour of how these schemes work by, again, taking Mark as an example. *RL*'s creators declared that it sees Mark's 'main interest' as 'the person of Jesus himself'. This is seen as progressively revealed in the text as the journey towards Jerusalem moves forward and as based on the climactic question 'who do men say that I am?' (Mark 8.29). It sees Peter's 'You are the Christ' as at 'the heart of Mark's Gospel'. In taking this position the Lectionary is following the mainstream of contemporary exegetical thinking about Mark – indeed since the Lectionary appeared there has been an increased emphasis among scholars on the need to view each Gospel as an entire unit

---

[3] All quotations are from the introduction to the 1982 edition of *RL*, xlvii.

as opposed to seeing them as quarries for the traditions that lie behind our texts.[4] The Lectionary then explains the inclusion of the 57 verses from John on Sundays 17 to 21[5] as adopting a single unit from John's 'sermon on the "Bread of Life"' which it sees as fitting 'well into [a particular] part of Mark's Gospel, which is concerned with Jesus' revelation of himself and is known as "the Bread section"'. And, as dovetailing of texts goes, this is about as neat as anything we might find: on Sunday 14 we have Mark 6.30–34 which is followed in the Gospel text (6.35–44) with the feeding miracle of the five loaves and the two fish, which is supplanted in the liturgical reading by John's imagery of bread, feeding and eating. The compilers do not explain the rationale for selecting John 18.33b–37 for Christ the King; but this to my mind is rather pleasant, for while in mathematics consistency is virtue, in theology its systematic invocation often spells death to that imaginative process without which faith is impossible.[6]

The scaffolding sees the 34 Sundays of Ordinary Time as being divisible into three units, each divided again into stages, and then with a key point for each Sunday's passage. So Mark is read as revealing the figure of Jesus the Messiah (unit 1), then 'the Mystery of Jesus' progressively revealed (unit 2), and then the Mystery of the Son of Man (unit 3). Unit 2, for example, is then seen as Jesus revealing himself to the Jewish crowds (stage 1), then to his disciples (stage 2), and then manifesting himself (stage 3). Then to take a Sunday within stage 2, e.g. Sunday 11: Mark 4.26–34, we have it described as 'Parables of the Kingdom'. It is this keynote that then acts as the criterion for which snippet of the Old Testament is chosen: Ezekiel 17.22–24.

While there are many minor differences between *RCL/CWL* and *RL* (> Appendix 3) – and despite *CWL* having other optional celebrations (e.g. 'Bible Sunday') – in so far as the Gospel forms the spine of the Liturgy of the Word, then the rationale for the selection of Gospels underlying the selection in *RL* also underlies *RCL* and *CWL*.

---

[4] See, for example, the essays in Bauckham 1998.

[5] *RL*'s numeration system will be followed as it is less cumbersome than that in *CWL*.

[6] Nor do they explain the choice of John 1.35–42 for Sunday 2.

Advent and Christmas

Christmas is our celebration of the mystery of the birth of Jesus the Lord (> O'Loughlin 2009a). Like all great moments it needs both a time of preparation, Advent, and a time to let it sink in: Christmastide. Together, the preparation and the time around and just after Christmas form the most recognizable period in the Christian year. Even people with only a very hazy notion about Christianity know that Christmas is a Christian feast; and while we Christians *know* that Easter is the greater feast, Christmas *feels* like the bigger event and it stands out for us more.

Once we had begun to celebrate Christmas (> Bradshaw and Johnson 2011, 123–68), it was inevitable that we would have to have a 'run-up period' and thus we have Advent. Once we had Advent, it was inevitable that people would not just see it as a run-up, but would ask what it was 'for' – and so we have the various Advent themes such as recalling the time of the old covenant, recalling the waiting for the Anointed One, recalling our own sinfulness, and recalling that the Christ who came once in Bethlehem, comes among us today in the Church in word and sacrament, and will come again at the end as the judge of the living and the dead. So the period of Advent is, liturgically, a 'theme-rich environment'.

The same happened with Christmas: once we were celebrating the birth of Jesus, and naturally we used the infancy Gospels of Matthew and Luke as the core of our remembering, we began to celebrate all the events that are found surrounding the birth of Jesus.[7] So we celebrated his circumcision 'on the eighth day' with a feast on 1 January, the coming of the Wise Men (or Kings) on the feast of the Epiphany, and later the feast of the presentation in the Temple (2 February). So Christmastide is, liturgically, a 'memory-rich environment'. Consequently, the Lectionary makers had little scope for making choices: one has the Gospel that supplies the feast's 'historical

---

[7] But bear in mind that our memory is not just a combination of the two accounts, but larger still: just look at a crib with its ox and ass, while the astrologers of Matt. 2.1–12 have been transformed into kings named Caspar, Melchior and Balthasar.

basis' and the other readings were chosen to echo or draw out that Gospel text.

However, since we have far more suitable readings for these themes and events than we could use in one year, we have a cycle of three years of readings. The cycle of three years has the added advantage that it allows us to shift perspective on the mystery of the Lord's coming from year to year. This is of crucial importance for the Church, for one of the characteristics of the mystery of the encounter of God and humanity in Jesus is that no matter how many ways we reflect on it, we will always discover within it new depths of what it means to us and its implications for how we live as Christians.

So the basic rule for understanding the Lectionary in this season is to look at the time or event we are celebrating. For Advent we can set these themes as shown in Table 5.3.[8]

Table 5.3 Gospel themes of Advent

Sunday	Gospel theme	Old Testament theme	Epistle theme
First	The Lord's coming at the end of time	Prophecies about (1) the Messiah	Exhortations and proclamations
Second	John the Baptist	[the Christ] and	of the various
Third	John the Baptist	(2) about the	themes of Advent
Fourth	The events that prepared immediately for the birth of Jesus	Messianic Age. Readings from Isaiah have a special place in setting out this theme	

But one can only appreciate these choices in the context of the overall liturgy of the particular day, and note how each day has a particular flavour depending on whether it is Year A, B or C. Once we arrive at Christmas, the arrangement of readings is eclogadic – the most appropriate Gospel being chosen for the feast of the day.

---

[8] For the actual readings, > Appendix 1.

Lent and Easter

As with the readings for Advent and Christmas, so the readings for Lent and Easter were chosen to harmonize with the mystery or the events being celebrated.

When does Lent begin?

Lent prepares for Easter, but once that was a fixed element in annual experience there was a preparation for the preparation, resulting in 'Septuagesima', 'Sexagesima' and 'Quinquagesima' on the Sundays before Ash Wednesday. These have disappeared completely from *RL*, but have left a mark in *CWL* as the two Sundays before Lent (> Buxton 2002), and one Sunday in *RCL*. So in *CWL* these two Sundays have to be seen as outside the structure of Ordinary Time, but not yet Lent. There is no common theme over the three years for the Second Sunday before Lent, but the Sunday before Lent has that of the transfiguration, interpreted in the collects as a request for the grace to change our lives and obey the call 'to listen to him' (Matt. 17.5; Mark 9.7; Luke 9.35).

Lent

There are four guiding principles:

1 The Gospel read on each Sunday is the key reading.
2 The Old Testament readings have been chosen to harmonize with the Gospels.
3 The psalms have been chosen to provide a prayerful response to the Old Testament readings.
4 The epistle readings have been chosen 'to fit the gospel and Old Testament readings and, to the extent possible, to provide a connection between them'.

The Gospel themes are shown in Table 5.4 overleaf.[9]

---

[9] For the actual readings, > Appendix 2.

Table 5.4 Gospel themes of Lent

Sunday	Year A (Matthew)	Year B (Mark)	Year C (Luke)
First	Accounts of the Lord's temptation		
Second	*RL*: the transfiguration accounts; having used the transfiguration accounts on 1 BL, *RCL* and *CWL* have forewarnings of the Passion, but making the same point as *RL*: the Son of Man must suffer		
Third	The Samaritan Woman	Jesus cleansing the Temple	The call to repentance
Fourth	The man born blind	The Son of Man must be lifted up	Forgiveness as seen in the Prodigal Son parable
Fifth	The raising of Lazarus	The Son of Man is glorified	*RL*: Woman taken in adultery; *CWL*: Anointing at Bethany[10]
Palm Sunday	Matthew's Passion narrative	Mark's Passion narrative	Luke's Passion narrative

The Paschal Triduum

All the readings are related to the events being celebrated as seen from the perspective of the Church's memory of Jesus.

Eastertide

All the readings are related in some way to the theme of the risen Christ who is now present in the community.

---

[10] There is a long-standing hesitation in many quarters about reading John 7.53—8.11 (the '*pericope de adultera*') in the liturgy either because of its doubtful textual 'authority' or because it might lessen the seriousness of the need for penitence or because it would encourage immorality among women (> O'Loughlin 2000). These hesitations were finally banished by *RL* in 1969, but continue in *RCL* where this pericope is not read on any Sunday (in *CWL* it is only found as an option for Ash Wednesday (> Giles 2001, 233)). In *RL* it has become a favourite text for preaching (> O'Loughlin 2004, 108–12). *RCL*'s choice for this Sunday can be justified as a quasi-eclogadic element at this point in Lent; however, by retaining the other readings as in *RL*, the set of readings has lost coherence.

Gospels

On the first three Sundays the Gospels recount the appearances of the risen Christ. On the fourth Sunday, the theme of the Good Shepherd from John's Gospel is read. On the remaining Sundays, excerpts from 'the last supper discourse' in John are read.

First readings

These are taken from the Acts of the Apostles and over a three-year cycle are intended to show the life of the early churches. This selection from Acts focuses on the church in Jerusalem in its earliest days. It is one of the weaknesses of the entire Lectionary that the second half of Acts dealing with the travels of Paul and his church around the rim of the Mediterranean is nowhere read in the regular cycles of readings. These readings from Acts are not thematically linked to the Gospels, except in that both relate to the earliest days of the Church.

This is the only period in the year when the first readings on a Sunday are not from the Old Testament. However, *CWL* does present, as an option, a set of Old Testament readings for these Sundays; but it is not immediately obvious how these texts relate either to the liturgical season or to the day's Gospel.

Second readings

In Year A we read from 1 Peter; in Year B from 1 John; and in Year C we read from Revelation which, while it does fit with the time, is not nearly so snug a fit as the readings for Years A and B. These readings are not thematically linked to either the Gospels or first readings.

So, between Easter and Ascension we have three cycles of readings: Acts, second readings and Gospels, which are not related to one another, but all of which are seen as somehow suitable to the time. This presents preachers with a task that is unique in the whole liturgical year – and many of these are not very suitable for preaching the nature of Christian belief in the resurrection.

Ascension, Pentecost and after

All the readings are related to the memory of the day being celebrated. The same applies to the feasts, such as Trinity Sunday, which follow in the wake of Eastertide.

Ordinary Time A: year of Matthew

The fundamental dynamic is the semi-continuous reading of Matthew; and each Gospel reading determines its first reading from the Old Testament. There is a distinct series of semi-continuous Old Testament readings in *RCL* (> Appendix 5).[11] The second readings, 'epistles', form a distinct set of semi-continuous readings which, except by coincidence, are *not related to either of the other readings* (> Appendix 4).

The year of Matthew is envisaged by the Lectionary's designers as comprising seven units varying in length from just one Sunday (unit 7) to a lengthy sequence of nine Sundays (unit 6). The core of the year is the five great 'sermons' that go to make up Matthew's Gospel, and these form units 2–6, preceded by unit 1 on the figure of Jesus the Christ, and concluded by the last Sunday of the year focusing on the fulfilment of God's kingdom (unit 7). In this year each unit is made up of two types of text: some narrative (over one or more Sundays), then some discourse (always over more than one Sunday).

The five sermons are:

- the sermon on the mount (Sundays 4–9)
- the mission sermon (Sundays 11–13)
- the parable sermon (Sundays 15–17)
- the community sermon (Sundays 23–4) and
- the final sermon (Sundays 32–3).

As with all schematic division systems for the Gospels, it is neater in the abstract than in terms of actual lections chosen. However, it is worth bearing in mind the Lectionary's desire to respect, in so far as it can, the five-sermon structure of Matthew (outside of his infancy and Passion narratives – used at Christmas and Easter), as it often helps us to appreciate the rationale behind making the junctions occur where they do (and the slight variations in *RCL* and *CWL* do not alter this), and the choice of accompanying first reading, which often functions as a lens highlighting a particular aspect of the Gospel on a particular Sunday.

---

[11] Optional in *CWL*.

Lectionary unit 1

This consists of just two Sundays and focuses on the figure of Jesus the Messiah. The question, who is the Christ, is then explored with the story of Jesus' baptism (Sunday 1[12]) and the witness of John the Baptist (Sunday 2).

Lectionary unit 2

This unit comprises Sundays 3–9, and its focus is on Christ's design for life in God's kingdom. There is one Sunday devoted to narrative, Sunday 3, which highlights the call of the first disciples. The remaining Sundays' Gospels are seen as discourse, which together make up the sermon on the mount.

Lectionary unit 3

This unit covers Sundays 10–13, and its focus is on the spread of God's kingdom. There is one Sunday devoted to narrative, Sunday 10, which highlights the call of Levi. The remaining Sundays' Gospels are seen as discourse: the mission sermon.

Lectionary unit 4

This unit comprises Sundays 14–17, and its focus is on the mystery of God's kingdom. There is one Sunday devoted to narrative, Sunday 14, whose theme is the revelation to the simple. The remaining Sundays' Gospels are seen as discourse, which together make up the parable sermon.

Lectionary unit 5

This unit comprises Sundays 18–24, and its focus is on God's kingdom on earth – the Church of Christ. There are five Sundays devoted to narrative:

- Sunday 18: the feeding of the five thousand;
- Sunday 19: Jesus walking on water;
- Sunday 20: the healing/exorcism of the Canaanite woman's daughter;
- Sunday 21: Peter's confession of Jesus' identity (to which the Lectionary adds the comment 'the primacy conferred'); and
- Sunday 22: discipleship and the prophecy of the Passion.

---

[12] The *RL* numbering is used as it is less cumbersome, but all the details can be found in Appendix 3.

This set of five Sundays has less unity than the other units in this year's lectionary, and the sequence of three Sundays each with a miracle story poses its own difficulties. The remaining Sundays' Gospels (Sundays 23 and 24) are seen as discourse, the community sermon.

Lectionary unit 6

This unit comprises Sundays 25–33, and the Lectionary gives it the title of 'Authority and Invitation – the ministry ends'. However, it has far less unity of theme or focus than the other units. Seven Sundays are presented as devoted to narrative: Sundays 25–31; then Sundays 32 and 33 are presented as discourse: the final sermon. However, the narrative section begins with four Sundays on which parables are read (25–28); these are followed by three other elements which are located here as that is roughly where they fall in Matthew's Gospel read continuously. This unit's structure is an attempt to find a logic in Matthew's Gospel, after the fact; and its rationale of 'narrative followed by discourse' is artificial.

Lectionary unit 7

This unit consists of just one Sunday, Sunday 34, the Last Sunday of the Year; and the Lectionary describes its focus as 'God's kingdom fulfilled': the Son of Man coming in glory as Christ the King. The focus of the Sunday is the Matthaean presentation of Jesus as the King in judgement at the end of time. In this unit all three readings form a thematic unity; indeed in Year A the second reading and Gospel supply, together, all the basic imagery that underpins the Feast of Christ the King.

The overall plan for the year of Matthew is represented in Table 5.5.

Table 5.5 The year of Matthew in Ordinary Time

Unit	Type of Gospel	Sundays
1 The figure of Jesus the Messiah		1–2
2 Christ's design for life in God's kingdom	Narrative	3
	Discourse: the sermon on the mount	4–9
3 The spread of God's kingdom	Narrative	10
	Discourse: the mission sermon	11–13

Table 5.5 (continued)

Unit	Type of Gospel	Sundays
4 The mystery of God's kingdom	Narrative	14
	Discourse: the parable sermon	15–17
5 God's kingdom on earth – the Church of Christ	Narrative	18–22
	Discourse: the community sermon	23–24
6 Authority and invitation – the ministry ends	Narrative	25–31
	Discourse: the final sermon	32–33
7 God's kingdom fulfilled		34

Ordinary Time B: year of Mark

This year is based on the semi-continuous reading of Mark (apart from his Passion narrative, used at Easter), along with some passages from John. The same arrangements apply for the relationship of the Gospel to the other readings as in Year A.

The Lectionary is planned in three major units, and several 'stages' within these (see Table 5.6 overleaf).

Lectionary unit 1

This unit consists of just two Sundays which are seen to open the year and the Gospel by focusing on the figure of Jesus the Messiah. This is expressed on the Feast of the Baptism (Sunday 1) with Mark's account; and then the call of Andrew and his companion from John's Gospel (Sunday 2). The two events taken together provide the witness from heaven and earth to Jesus being the Promised One.

Lectionary unit 2.1

This unit consists of 21 Sundays whose overall theme is the mystery of Jesus being progressively revealed. It is made up of three stages:

1 Jesus with the Jewish crowds
2 Jesus with his disciples
3 Jesus' manifestation of himself.

Table 5.6 The year of Mark: Ordinary Time

Unit	Stage	Sundays
1 The figure of Jesus the Messiah		1–2
2 The mystery progressively revealed	1 Jesus with the Jewish crowds	3–9
	2 Jesus with his disciples	10–14
	3 Jesus manifests himself	15–23
3 The mystery of the Son of Man	1 The 'way' of the Son of Man	24–30
	2 Final revelation in Jerusalem	31–33
	3 The fulfilment of the mystery	34

The first stage runs from the third to the ninth Sunday. In these Gospels we encounter Jesus around the Sea of Galilee, healing a leper and a paralytic, and answering questions about fasting and the Sabbath.

Lectionary unit 2.2

The second stage of this unit, which is concerned with the mystery of Jesus being progressively revealed, focuses on Jesus with his disciples. This stage runs from the tenth to the fourteenth Sunday. In these Gospels we encounter Jesus facing serious criticism, preaching parables of the kingdom, calming the storm, healing and being rejected at Nazareth.

Lectionary unit 2.3

This stage of the second unit (whose overall theme is the mystery of Jesus being progressively revealed) focuses on Jesus' manifestation of himself. This stage is unusual in the Lectionary for Ordinary Time in that it is made up of sections from John as well as Mark. It begins with two Sundays (15 and 16) where Jesus gives the Twelve their mission and then manifests compassion on the crowds. This mention of crowds around Jesus is then the cue for a five-Sunday selection from John 6 on the Eucharist. The stage then concludes with two more Gospel readings from Mark on Sundays 22 and 23.

Lectionary unit 3.1

This unit consists of 11 Sundays (Sundays 24 to 34 inclusive) whose overall theme is the mystery of the Son of Man. It is made up of three units:

1 the 'way' of the Son of Man
2 the final revelation in Jerusalem
3 the fulfilment of the mystery.

The first stage runs from the twenty-fourth to the thirtieth Sunday. It opens with Peter's confession of faith and then the narrative that immediately follows in Mark.

Lectionary unit 3.2

This stage consists of three Sundays (Sundays 31 to 33 inclusive) when we read of the final revelation of the identity of the Son of Man in Jerusalem.

Lectionary unit 3.3

This stage consists of the last Sunday of Ordinary Time, when the Feast of Christ the King is seen as the liturgical celebration of the fulfilment of the mystery of the Son of Man. Although this is seen as the culmination of the Year of Mark, the end of the year's reflection on the eschaton is taken from John.

Ordinary Time C: year of Luke

The basis of this year is the semi-continuous reading of Luke (apart from the infancy narrative and the Passion narrative used at Christmas and Easter). The same arrangements apply for the relationship of the Gospel to the other readings as in Year A. The Year of Luke is envisaged by the Lectionary as comprising eight units ranging in length from one Sunday (units 5 and 8) to eleven Sundays (unit 4).

We can see Luke's agenda as broadly geographical and spread over his two works: the Gospel and Acts.

Jesus travels from
Nazareth to Jerusalem and death and resurrection and his return to
the Father.
The Church travels from
Jerusalem to the Earth's ends through suffering and death to glory.

The Lectionary consciously adopts this theme, and Luke's travel narrative (chapters 9—19) provides the readings for the core of Ordinary Time: Sundays 13–31. This journey is more chronological in structure than geographical, and so is well suited to being read sequentially in time, Sunday after Sunday. The journey is also assumed to parallel the journey of the People of God, both collectively and as individuals, for it is the journey through life's sufferings and joys. The Lectionary expects that each Sunday will be seen in the light of the larger units (groups of Sundays) and the whole journey theme.

Lectionary unit 1: Jesus the Christ

This consists of just two Sundays and focuses on the figure of Jesus the Messiah. The question, who is the Christ, is then explored with the story of Jesus' baptism (Sunday 1) and the manifestation of his glory at the wedding in Cana (Sunday 2).

Lectionary unit 2: Luke's programme

The second unit is made up of two Sundays with a common theme – indeed they share a single narrative section of the Gospel – which is Luke's programme for the ministry of Jesus. It consists of Sundays 3 and 4, both of which focus on Jesus' visit to the synagogue in Nazareth. These two Sundays (with the prologue and Jesus' identification of himself as the one fulfilling the prophecy of Isaiah) set the tone for the year: the Jubilee Year has come and with it a new relationship of righteousness between God and his people, and so a new relationship of justice among God's people is called for.

Lectionary unit 3: Galilee

This unit is devoted to Jesus' ministry in Galilee. It runs from Sunday 5 to Sunday 12, and contains seven or eight Sundays depending on whether a particular year has 33 or 34 Sundays in total. This is probably the least useful unit from the standpoint of preaching or teaching as it is always broken up by the period of Lent-Eastertide-Trinity.

Its sections and themes are shown in Table 5.7.

Table 5.7 The year of Luke: Ordinary Time Sundays 5–12

Sunday 5	*The call of the first apostles*
Sunday 6	The sermon on the plain (1)
Sunday 7	The sermon on the plain (2)
Sunday 8	The sermon on the plain (3)
Sunday 9	Curing the centurion's servant
Sunday 10	*The widow at Naim (NRSV Nain)*
Sunday 11	*The woman anoints Jesus' feet*
Sunday 12	Peter's confession of faith

The sections of the Gospel referred to in *italics* in this chart are incidents that are only found in Luke's Gospel and so are texts that are only preached upon on these Sundays in the three-year cycle, whereas the Lucan texts on the other Sundays may be verbally very similar to texts met elsewhere in the Gospels and consequently read on other Sundays over the three years.

Lectionary unit 4: towards Jerusalem

This unit is devoted to the first part of the 'travel narrative' and its theme is the qualities Jesus demands of those who follow him. It runs from Sunday 13 to Sunday 23, and contains 11 Sundays. Its sections and themes are shown in Table 5.8.

Table 5.8 The year of Luke: Ordinary Time Sundays 13–23

Sunday 13	*The journey begins*
Sunday 14	*The mission of the seventy-two*
Sunday 15	*The Good Samaritan*
Sunday 16	*At the meal in the house of Martha and Mary*
Sunday 17	*The friend in need*
Sunday 18	*The parable of the rich fool building barns*
Sunday 19	The need for vigilance
Sunday 20	Jesus brings 'not peace but division'
Sunday 21	Few will be saved
Sunday 22	True humility
Sunday 23	The cost of discipleship

Lectionary unit 5: pardon and reconciliation

This unit consists of just one Sunday: Sunday 24. Its focus is on the 'gospel within the Gospel': Jesus' message of pardon and reconciliation. It is devoted to Luke 15 (all but three verses of which are only found in this Gospel), which consists of a string of three parables: the lost coin; the lost sheep; and the prodigal son.

Lectionary unit 6: towards Jerusalem, again

This unit is devoted to the second part of the 'travel narrative' and explores the obstacles facing those who follow Jesus. It runs from Sunday 25 to Sunday 31; its sections and themes are shown in Table 5.9.

Table 5.9 The year of Luke: Ordinary Time Sundays 25–31

Sunday 25	*The unjust steward*
Sunday 26	*The rich man and Lazarus*
Sunday 27	*A lesson on faith and dedication*
Sunday 28	*The ten lepers*
Sunday 29	*The unjust judge*
Sunday 30	*The Pharisee and the tax-collector*
Sunday 31	*Meeting Zacchaeus*

In many ways this is the most characteristic section of Luke's Gospel, for none of these sections, stories or incidents are found elsewhere in the Gospels.

Lectionary unit 7: the ministry in Jerusalem

This unit is devoted to Jesus' ministry in Jerusalem. It consists of just Sunday 32 and Sunday 33; and it has an eschatological theme running through it. On Sunday 32 we have the debate about the nature of the resurrection; and then on Sunday 33 we have 'the signs' announcing the End.

Lectionary unit 8: the Christ is King – reconciliation

This unit consists of just one Sunday: Sunday 34, the Last Sunday of the Year. The focus is upon reconciliation and this is expressed through reading the account of the repentant thief from the Passion narrative. This story is only found in Luke's Gospel.

When we present it in tabulated form (see Table 5.10) we see just how much of the material in this year would otherwise go unheard in the Sunday liturgy.

Table 5.10 The year of Luke, Ordinary Time: Gospel material peculiar to Luke

Unit	Note	Sunday
1 The figure of Jesus the		1
Messiah		2
2 Luke's programme for		3
Jesus' ministry		4
3 The Galilean ministry		5
		6
		7
		8
		9
	found only in Luke	10
	found only in Luke	11
		12
4 The first part of the 'travel	*found only in Luke*	13
narrative': the qualities Jesus	*found only in Luke*	14
demands in his followers	*found only in Luke*	15
	found only in Luke	16
	found only in Luke	17
	found only in Luke	18
		19
		20
		21
		22
		23
5 The 'Gospel within the Gospel':	*found only in Luke*	24
Pardon and reconciliation		
6 The second part of the 'travel	*found only in Luke*	25
narrative': the obstacles facing	*found only in Luke*	26
those who follow Jesus	*found only in Luke*	27
	found only in Luke	28
	found only in Luke	29
	found only in Luke	30
	found only in Luke	31
7 The ministry in Jerusalem		32
		33
8 Christ the King: reconciliation	*found only in Luke*	34

The bird's-eye view

Encountered, as it is in the liturgy, in chunks week by week, the Lectionary seems like a jumble of extracts from which we are expected to squeeze some value as each passage comes along. Seen in terms of its overall plan – allowing that there have to be compromises – the present Lectionary appears to be one of the most concerted efforts to set out the kerygma in our history. Through it the preaching of the evangelists has been made available for our regular meal-assemblies in a way that respects their separate Gospels, while also taking account of the need to present the story of the Christ-event within the unfolding of the Christian year. The adage, 'the whole is greater than the sum of the parts', applies to it: only when we see the architecture of the whole, do we see why the parts are located as they are.

6

Appreciating the Lectionary: plus and minus

If you have worked your way through to this point, you probably are prepared to accept these conclusions:

- that lectionaries hold an important place in worship and in the Christian life to the extent that one sees taking part in the liturgy as a central part of discipleship;
- that creating a lectionary is not the simple business of 'picking suitable passages' but a complex work involving the nature of Christian tradition, the nature of the liturgy, and how we celebrate and communicate – therefore, it involves delicate acts of balancing various factors and making necessary compromises; and
- that the present Lectionary resulted from a deliberate process unparalleled in Christian history in its conscious attempts to relate the inheritance of the Gospels, and the rest of the Scriptures, to the situation of the liturgy.

Once one acknowledges the difficulties involved in this task, it may seem churlish to set out the good and bad points of the Lectionary, but it is also worthwhile to take stock.

The reception of the Lectionary

A first, and obvious, comment must be that while the Lectionary did not attract the fiery criticism of those who were opposed to the reformed liturgy that emerged in the aftermath of Vatican II – and the Lectionary was fully part of that reform (> Bugnini 1990, 406–25) – neither has it generated, among Catholics at least, a great circle of friends and admirers. The Lectionary seems to be 'just there' and it is followed because it is there, but without any particular enthusiasm. This lack of appreciation can be seen from the fact that I have not heard any sense of loss when chopping and changing interrupts and destroys its overall plan of the use of the Gospels in the liturgy. This was probably due, mainly, to the fact that among Catholics the notion of paying attention to the Liturgy of the Word was itself so new in the aftermath of the Council that it was, first, the *fact* of a prominent Liturgy of the Word, second, that it was in the vernacular, and third, that it was actually addressed to the gathering, rather than its *arrangement* that was the source of wonder. In a sense, any vernacular lectionary would have done: the fact was that now people were expected to listen to the Scriptures at the Eucharist. When Latin ceased to be a living language in the West is a complicated question beyond the scope of this book, but suffice to say that by 820 there was little likelihood that anyone – even a cleric fluent in Latin – would *hear* the readings and understand them at anything other than the most special occasions when they were sung aloud. The normal experience was that of the 'Low Mass' where, facing the book, and with his back to those present, the priest read both epistle and Gospel in a low, almost inaudible voice, and the only outward mark of this part of the liturgy was that the server moved the book from one side of the altar to the other – a vestigial memory of a time when many ministers were needed for any celebration. This silent 'liturgy of the word' only began to change in 1961 when, on certain occasions, after being read in Latin, it was permitted to repeat them in translation (> Seasoltz 1966, 453).[1] So when less than a decade later Latin had virtually disappeared from Roman liturgy, it was these visible facts about the Liturgy of the Word, rather than the structure of the Lectionary, that

---

[1] A curious false memory has grown up among Catholics apologetic for the Tridentine rite to the effect that the readings were always bilingual – this is simply not the case: the 1961 permission was the first time that the place of Latin in the eucharistic liturgy was challenged – and even then only in a very limited way; the other false memory is that 'people followed the readings in their [people's] missals' – but this ignores these facts: (1) that vernacular missals were strongly discouraged until the early twentieth century as likely to weaken objections to the Protestant practice of having a vernacular liturgy; (2) they were expensive and so comparatively rare; and (3) finding the right passage, and then reading it alone in silence, implied a skill and dedication beyond all but a very small, liturgically aware, elite: most who had missals used them as 'prayer books' and most of those books supplied pious and diverting activities to occupy the minds of their owners during those periods of the Mass when 'nothing was happening' (i.e. during the readings).

grabbed attention (> O'Loughlin 2010a). Moreover, the Liturgy of the Word had such a minimal profile in thinking about the Eucharist (it was referred to as the 'Mass of the Catechumens' as distinct from 'the Mass of the Faithful' with the implication that it was unproblematic and rather simple in comparison with the 'Mass proper' (> Croegaert 1958)), that it was interest in the changes to the eucharistic ritual which absorbed energy rather than anything connected with the Scriptures. For Catholics the big change was not the new Lectionary, but hearing readings in English or whatever was the language of their home and street.

This lack of interest in, not to mention admiration of, the Lectionary persists today. While all clergy know there is a three-year cycle of readings, few can elaborate its rationale; and this lack of interest is then transmitted to the rest of the church. Moreover, there is little likelihood of this changing in that each year groups of bishops approve other celebrations for Sundays or move other feasts on to Sundays, each with their own readings, which suggests that they do not see the programme of the Lectionary as something to value, preserve or promote. This process not only desacralizes time apart from Sundays, but assumes that there is little of value lost when the Lectionary's overall plan is made impossible. Meanwhile, the internal logic of the Lectionary can come as a revelation to many priests. Faced with a genuine pastoral need to omit a reading, the most common decision one encounters is that of 'dropping' the first reading – indicative of a more general lack of concern for reading the Old Testament. The notion that the first reading might be the one with the link to the Gospel seems alien, while many struggle each week to see how all three readings, or, at least, the epistle and Gospel, are related. It is worth noting that in the Tridentine and BCP Lectionary there was no connection, outside of the seasons, between the epistle and the Gospel (> Appendix 6).

By contrast, the churches of the Reformation have been far more appreciative of *RL*. Long familiar with vernacular lectionaries – indeed seen as part of the *raison d'être* – which were actually read to the congregation, they looked at the Lectionary and saw neither the fact nor the language, but the arrangement, and the benefits that might result from tackling the fundamental issues involved in lectionaries head on. The result has been the three-year-cycle Lectionaries we know as *RCL* (1992) and *CWL* (1999). Because these three Lectionaries can be seen as forming a textual family, the latter two are often presented as simply 'copies, with amendments' of *RL*, but such comments fail to do justice to the care and work of the various groups responsible for revising the Lectionary in various churches (> Hageman 1982; West 1997, ix–xi; Hebblethwaite 2004, 14–16), nor to the fact that some of them were thinking of revising their lectionaries since the 1940s. Rather than seeing this convergence in terms of borrowing from one another, it is better to see it as independent responses to a common task – to have a lectionary suitable for the Eucharist – which admits only a certain number of solutions, and if one comes up with a similar solution, then one might as well adopt one's neighbour's lectionary as this brings the additional benefit of ecumenical convergence. Given how contemporary theologians speak of the role of the Word in liturgy, and in particular at a celebration of the Eucharist, then it is very hard to avoid the set of choices that faced those who produced *RL* (> Bonneau 1998, 31–55). It follows, therefore, that there are benefits in adopting similar solutions on the broad level, with the way these compromises have to be negotiated resulting in more variations at the level of what is read on particular days. These differences range from issues about where a particular unit within the biblical texts begins or ends – note the frequency with which one lectionary begins or ends at verse 1a or 2, while the other opts for the opposite – to cases where doctrinal concerns determined the reading: anyone reading Matthew appreciates that his account of the promise of the Messiah ends sharply with 1.25 (> *RCL/CWL*, 4 Advent, Year A); however, that verse is problematic for Catholics who suspect that it could imply that Matthew did not think of Mary as 'ever-virgin', so it does not occur in the Lectionary.[2] So while this lectionary family has a common core – the sequences of Gospel readings – and then levels of variation as these were adapted to distinct calendars, in so far as they differ (e.g., *CWL* makes provision for celebrations such as Bible Sunday), to churches' traditions of worship (e.g., *RCL/CWL* supposes much greater familiarity with

---

[2] Whether or not Matt. 1.25 does imply that not all 'sources of revelation' are in agreement is not my concern (> McHugh 1975, 204 for a standard Catholic explanation), but that it was sufficiently worrying to the Lectionary's creators that they omitted it.

the use of the Psalms than *RL*), and to particular concerns over the nature of the Scriptures (e.g. readings from what some would deem 'apocrypha' are omitted in *RCL* and have 'canonical' alternatives in *CWL*). Moreover, while it would be true to say that, in general, the Ministry of the Word has a higher prominence at eucharistic celebration in Protestant churches than the Liturgy of the Word among Catholics, it is not the case that there is greater awareness of the architecture of the Lectionary. This can be seen in several ways. There is a far greater willingness to abandon the Lectionary in favour of a preacher's chosen texts which prioritize the sermon rather than the Scriptures. The practice of moving between rites among Anglicans (*Common Worship* one week, BCP another, and perhaps *ASB* on another) makes any consistent exploitation of the Lectionary impossible; while one has sympathy with the guest preacher who, arriving to preach with a homily based on *CWL*, found BCP being used – she graciously admitted the crossed wires and retold from memory the scene on which her homily was based, which had the effect of focusing her audience more than ever!

Right across the range of churches using the Lectionary there is a persistent attitude that a lectionary is just a convenient album of biblical texts. So for all concerned it is a book waiting to be discovered. Consequently, providing training in using the Lectionary is one of the major challenges facing liturgical renewal.

Fare for 'the table of the word'

On the 'plus' side one cannot but be struck by how well the Lectionary has fulfilled the tasks set by the various churches when they embarked on the process of reforming their Lectionaries. Anyone looking at the Lectionaries replaced by *RL* and *CWL* (> Appendix 6) can quickly identify their two salient features. First, the overall paucity of texts – albeit in the Protestant churches these were actually heard, and heard in the vernacular. And second, the eclogadic elements around the great festivals apart, the texts occur in no particular order. In fact, the old Lectionaries are a jumble without an overall plan (there was a vestigial nod to 'continuous reading') or even a convenient arrangement. This was no better for the BCP than for the Missal of Trent; after all both Lectionaries were closely related historically, and they ran in a kind of 'wrinkled parallel'.[3]

So how did it come about that the old Lectionary was left completely aside? After all, one of the curious features of human ritual behaviour is that no matter how inherently perverse an element of ritual is, usually as a result of historical accidents, once it has been used, it becomes immovable (> O'Loughlin 2009). Then, instead of seeing blunders and confusions, one hears of vague phrases such as 'usage hallowed by the use of generations' or encounters individualist aesthetic judgements as a substitute for theological understanding. Such rearguard defences were mounted time and again at Vatican II (and with growing ferocity ever since), and there are analogous movements in other churches. However, while Catholics were not the first to broach the questions of lectionary reform, it was one of the topics to which, early on (4 December 1963), the Council committed itself to action:

> The treasures of the Bible are to be opened up more lavishly so that a richer fare may be provided for the faithful at the table of God's word. In this way a more representative part of the sacred scriptures will be read to the people in the course of a prescribed number of years. (*SC*, 1)

And:

> a more ample, more varied, and more suitable reading from sacred scripture should be restored. (*SC*, 35)

In the face of this public recognition of the limitations of the existing Lectionary, and a clear mandate for a bigger and better set of readings, the old disappeared almost without a whimper.[4] Not only was the fare on 'the table of the word' now to be more varied and ample, but it was

---

[3] They fell out of concordance when, on some occasion, a set of epistles were copied from one book (that of the subdeacon: the '*epistolarium*') while the Gospels were copied from another (that used by the deacon: the '*evangelarium*') when these two books had not been correctly aligned with one another and the calendar.

[4] Moreover, the Lectionary benefited from the sad irony that the readings were regarded with such minimal interest before the Council, that those who were concerned with the 'innovations' of the reformed rite paid hardly any attention to this part of the reform!

to be presented from a very particular point of view, itself embedded within the renewed Catholic understanding of the liturgy:

> The basic principle is that 'the mystery of Christ and the history of salvation' must be presented in the readings. Therefore, the new system must contain the whole nucleus of the apostolic preaching about Jesus as 'Lord and Christ' (Acts 2:36) who fulfilled the Scriptures by his life, his preaching, and, above all, his paschal mystery and who gives life to the Church until his glorious return.   (> Bugnini 1990, 410)

This was the starting point that led in a period of less than five years to *RL*.

Anglicans' experience with regard to lectionary renewal is rather different (> Giles 2001). On the one hand, because the Lectionary was part and parcel of that talisman of identity, the traditional Book of Common Prayer, in the desire to keep, defend, preserve that book – and the movement draws support from many people with only a peripheral interest in the dynamics of what is distinctive about Christian worship – they have defended its Lectionary also. Or, to put it another way, they have been so concerned with the BCP that they have not explored nor appreciated *Common Worship*, including one of its richest elements, its Lectionary. That said, while the BCP's Lectionary for the Eucharist was rather limited, in so far as other services such as Matins and Evensong were often the preferred principal Sunday liturgy, they had a long experience with a rich and varied lectionary (> Giles 2001, 227), to which was added twenty years' experience with the Lectionary of the *ASB*. They have also benefited from being the last to produce a lectionary with the modern lectionary family. If *RCL* can be seen to address some of the problems of *RL* – while also adapting it in other ways – then *CWL* was able to take advantage of both. The most significant example of this is the choice it offers between the two strategies for using the Old Testament in Ordinary Time found in *RL* and *RCL*. But this comment by Gordon Giles deserves attention:

> It is not in the spirit of the Lectionary to pick and choose between [those strategies], or between Old and New Testament lessons. Therefore preachers and leaders need to think ahead and plan what is to be read over many months.[5]

---

[5] Giles 2001, 231.

Perhaps this quotation should be made into a sticker and stuck up in sacristies and vestries as well as on lecterns, ambos and pulpits!

The situation is more varied among other churches that have adopted or, in some cases, have 'taken to using' the Lectionary. Part of the liturgical understanding of many of these churches was that they were supposedly free from constraints of books and formulae on their forms and expressions of worship (> Mitchell 1977, 97–114; McLuhan 1962, 137–41). In fact, humans develop patterns of behaviour such that this 'freedom' is always circumscribed by prior expectations and this forms the basis for all human ritual, religious or otherwise (> Rothenbuhler 1998, 123–8). When this approach to liturgy interacts with the question of what texts are read it becomes a fundamental matter that the congregation chooses the passages for worship. This becomes part of their self-identity and the basic premise in their scriptural hermeneutics (> West 1997, 65–70). As such, a lectionary is not only a new concept, but a potentially threatening and destabilizing one. The result is that the Lectionary is often partially adopted. It clearly has advantages if Christmas and Easter are being celebrated, while in many congregations during the rest of the year it is sometimes used and sometimes not. Again, this is the 'album of passages' approach. If the Lectionary is to be of any value, over and above the value of reading a passage of Scripture in worship, then that value lies in using it consistently over a period – it is only then that 'the whole' confers benefits over and above that of 'the parts'. Once again, the Lectionary is part of the wider renewal of worship and discovering its possibilities can often offer a balance to inherited fears (> Lathrop 2003, 143–4).

The Lectionary and *didachē*[6]

Throughout this book I have used the word 'reading' when referring to a passage of Scripture laid out in the Lectionary, while carefully avoiding the commonly used term 'lesson' as in: 'he read the lesson at the service' or 'nine lessons and carols'. This practice I have adopted

---

[6] The term *didachē* is usually rendered as 'teaching' but this is an overly academic translation – it is better seen as something like 'training' or 'instruction' – it is a practical activity aimed at forming a fully fledged disciple (> O'Loughlin 2011).

because in our culture, despite its good liturgical origin, the word 'lesson'[7] belongs to the world of education and the classroom rather than the world of liturgy and celebration. Our liturgy runs the constant danger of being seen as simply an educational event with activities – the ritual elements – or a class 'using symbols'; while the Liturgy of the Word, in particular, runs the risk of becoming a gathering for Scripture study. This is a failure to grasp the different formal objectives of three interconnected aspects of disciples – which have had distinct names throughout Christian history: *leitourgeia* where the focus is on the Israel – the church as community – blessing the Father; *didachē* which is the training and formation of individuals within the inheritance of the covenant community; and *kerugma* which is the proclamation and witness of the community to itself and before the world. They feed and support one another, and should never exist apart, but likewise should not be blurred. We can imagine them as in Figure 3.

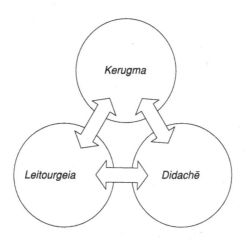

Figure 3

When we distinguish in this way, it becomes clear that the Lectionary must not only be an *object* of *didachē* or training – people must have a sense of what they are hearing in the liturgy and why – but also an

---

instrument of *didachē*. Here is a real benefit of the modern Lectionary. In most cases, one can explain why a particular reading has been chosen and placed in this position in the overall plan. One may disagree with all or parts of the rationale, but one cannot deny that the plan exists; and this plan can be set forth as one that was chosen because it was sensitive to the nature of the Gospels, the place of the various other parts of the Scriptures within Christianity, and the needs of worship. Likewise, the Lectionary's various plans within a year and over the three-year cycle – particularly since it is focused on the person and work of Jesus – can then be used as the basis for a diversity of catechetical and Bible-study plans. The liturgy, thereby, feeds growth in Christian awareness, and vice versa. So while it is a mistake to think of the Liturgy of the Word as a Bible-study class or catechetical event, the Lectionary can provide a valuable structure for such programmes so that they can run in parallel with the liturgy. For many Christians, and certainly for all Catholics, the arrival of the new Lectionary has ushered in the possibility of a formal paralleling of liturgy and catechesis such as had not existed in Western Latin Christianity since the fifth or sixth centuries. It is worth recalling that it was that experience of the parallel – not the fusion – of the liturgy with the instruction that resulted in some of the great cycles of exegetical and catechetical sermons of the Greek and Latin Fathers. Such a real link became impossible when the liturgy continued in Latin, the Lectionary lost coherence (as did the calendar), and instruction ceased to be based on hearing the Gospels (> Sloyan 1987). For a variety of reasons that link of exegesis and liturgy was not restored at the Reformation when liturgy was downplayed in comparison with reading, exegesis and instruction. Today, for the first time in over a millennium, the possibility of a balance lies before us – and a first step is to value our Lectionary more highly.

The Lectionary as an ecumenical event

When Vatican II commanded a revision of the Lectionary it did so against an awareness within Catholicism that something better had to be provided than what was then current and – as we noted above – there were already calls that the Scriptures should be actually read to the congregation. But the Council also consciously acted in the knowledge that many other churches were experimenting with new lectionaries that broke clear of the medieval model that had been widely retained, with only minor modifications (> Appendix 6), at the Reformation. These moves towards a new lectionary were afoot among Anglicans and others in Britain (> Hageman 1982), among Lutherans in Germany, Switzerland and Denmark, among other German Protestant churches, and in the Reformed Church in France. Some of these churches had already adopted a new lectionary – that of the Reformed Church in France, adopted in 1953, holds the title for being the first to use a system of three readings and spread the Lectionary over three years – while others were running experimental or optional lectionaries alongside their traditional ones (> Bugnini 1990, 416). Moreover, despite deep-seated differences regarding the hermeneutics of how Scripture functions in the Church (> West 1997), there was growing convergence about how it functioned in liturgy and in terms of human communication. Indeed, it was Marshall McLuhan, the great theorist of how the media works, who pointed out in 1962 that all the churches were finding the advent of the electronic age was forcing them to reflect on liturgical patterns which, he believed, had their genesis in the individualistic piety of the later Middle Ages:

> It might baffle many to explain why there should be such a profound liturgical revival in our time, unless they are aware of the essentially oral character of the electric 'field'. Today there is a 'High Church' movement within Presbyterianism as well as in many other sects. The merely individual and visual aspects of worship no longer satisfy.[8]

So it perhaps was not as surprising as some have found it, that *RL* from its first appearance as a list of references in 1969 was being taken up by others. Giles summarizes thus: 'From about 1970, and unexpectedly, this lectionary began to be appropriated by some Anglican and Protestant churches, including the United Church of Canada and the United Methodist Church of the USA.'[9] And from this usage came, after reflection, experimentation and road testing

---

[8] McLuhan 1962, 137–8; this chapter of McLuhan is rarely noted by liturgists, yet its analysis, particularly of the situation in Catholic liturgy, is even more relevant today – when most people come to church with at least one bit of electronic technology in their pocket – than when he wrote it.

[9] Giles 2001, 230.

with three uses of the three-year cycle (= 9 years), the official launch of the *Revised Common Lectionary* in 1992, which can be seen as the immediate parent of *CWL*. While many have been amazed at the speed with which the group of experts formed after Vatican II produced *RL*, one has to be equally amazed at the care and deliberation that went into *RCL*.

While in every church there are those who see 'ecumenism' as 'selling out' (or worse), by and large those who are interested in lectionaries see this ecumenical dimension as one of its positive advantages – though Catholics are perhaps least aware of this impact of the reform of their liturgy in the 1960s beyond their boundaries. Clearly, when churches do together what they can do together, it can be seen as one more step on the road to Christian harmony, as well as having practical benefits. Likewise, the more that churches learn to learn from one another (and as *RCL* learned from *RL*, *RCL* now has a lot to teach *RL*), the greater the level of mutual understanding and respect, both of which are prerequisites for common witness to Jesus. However, there are two important lessons in the fact that such widely differing churches have adopted this Lectionary: first, the nature of liturgy is closely linked to our humanity – how we recall, how we memorialize, how we celebrate – and this undercuts differences that often emerged in theologians' studies; and, second, the challenges of communication and interpretation are common to all who claim that texts produced in ancient, and alien, societies can still be vehicles of the Spirit for communities today.

The problem of training and catechesis

Part of taking stock of where we are with regard to the Lectionary is to note the problems that have arisen or that have been ignored. When *RL* appeared, its introduction was explicit that it would make wholly new demands on clergy and that it would only bear fruit after extensive training – indeed one of the arguments made against its introduction was that Catholic priests would not have the skills it presupposed, while training future clergy in its use would make heavy demands on seminaries (> Bugnini 1990, 415). In many other documents this need for specialist training both in the nature of the Liturgy of the Word *as liturgy* and in using the Scriptures *in liturgy* and in preaching *within liturgy* has been stressed repeatedly ever since.

Similar expressions of the need for training are contained in the documents of other churches, and their very repetition suggests that they are not being acted on! The simple fact is that the Lectionary, in consciously seeking to return to a situation modelled on the liturgy and practice of Ambrose and Augustine, among the Latins, has presented clergy with a task that has *not occurred in any Western church* for more than a millennium – and that level of skill will not be built up quickly.

Alas, when one looks over the academic programmes of seminaries and theological colleges across the denominational spectrum, one finds invariably biblical studies (quantity and status vary across churches), liturgical studies (sometimes simply 'how to' instructions), and homiletics or communications (varying according to resources and whether they see themselves as centres of 'theological training' or 'pastoral formation'), but the special tasks that a commitment to this Lectionary imposes upon ministers are only matters of incidental comments.

The situation in most churches is summed up in these two anecdotes. When I asked a recently ordained Anglican how she found *CWL* she replied that it was used in the churches in which she ministered, and she liked the idea of a lectionary because she thought it was a convenient way of allowing everyone involved in the liturgy to know what was going to be read. Which Old Testament system did she use between Trinity and Advent? In two of her churches she said that they only read the epistle (*sic*) and the Gospel as these services had to take place within a limited time, while in the third church they used the *RCL* strategy. When I asked if this was a preference for *RCL* or a preference against the *RL* strategy, she told me that she had never considered the matter as the choice was made by the lady who drew up the readers' rota – and she could not see any reason to disturb the system; and one suspects that the lady concerned drew on *RCL* readings simply because they came first in the book! My second anecdote concerns Catholic clergy and my amazement that a friend was able to report a full house at his lecture on using the Lectionary in Lent. So I asked for his secret. The answer is self-explanatory. Either arrange the time of one's lecture between that of a canon lawyer and the time of a meal or, if the bishop is attending, arrange to speak immediately after him – if he stays for the lecture, then so will everyone else! If clergy are having problems making room for this new Christian event, then it is even more problematic for everyone else. In effect, this great monument of the Church of the twentieth century is being obscured – and being lost – through the friction and noise that inevitably accompany change.

The problem of diverging expectations

One specific aspect of more general lack of appreciation of the Lectionary is the divergence of expectations about the purpose of reading Scripture as part of the liturgy. Even if we leave aside different attitudes to the Scriptures per se (> West 1997, 47–58), there is the variety of expectations of what 'one can get out of the readings' that is part and parcel of postmodernity. One of the underlying principles of all lectionaries, and especially the modern Lectionary, is that the audience – literally the listening group – share a collective memory. This memory binds them together as a shared past (not just memory of Jesus 'as Lord and Christ', but the earlier memories that the Christ-event supposes – the Old Testament, and the memories of the community of the church) and gives them a shared vision of the future (not just eschatologically, but in terms of how they should and will act in their immediate situation). The Liturgy of the Word can, indeed, be seen as the 'remembering' component of the larger action of blessing God for his goodness that is the Eucharist – the whole event following the pattern of a classic prayer in the *berakah* form. But it is precisely the significance of the collective memory that creates communities and identities (> Schwartz 1982) that is challenged in the postmodern situation (> Spinks 2010). So for one the memory of Israel is a tale of God's loving purposes, but for another it is a jumble of details, for history has ceased to exist as an existential element in her or his life. Likewise, while one person may be waiting for the very words of Jesus their 'personal saviour', another wants a word of wisdom that might inspire reflection.

It is easy to lose heart when the postmodern condition is identified as part of the noise in which the gospel today must be heard, but one should set the situation in perspective. First, we confront the situation today with probably the finest Lectionary any church has had for centuries. It is not perfect – it is a human work in time – but it is far better than any of the other schemes that have been proposed. Second, every act of communication – a set of readings, a homily, the whole Liturgy of the Word – 'makes claims about how the world works and how we ought to work in it'.[10] Liturgy is not some sort of passive analysis of diagnosed problems, but a creative activity. It seeks to imagine the universe as God's cosmos: created, loved, redeemed, inspired. In imagining this world, it further helps all who participate in the liturgy to a similar act of imagination – and in so imagining, the kingdom is brought closer. The task for the community, and so especially for any who lead worship, is to make sure that the Liturgy of the Word – for which the Lectionary provides a skeleton – is a truly creative and imaginative event: making claims about the world as God's loved creation and proclaiming how, in collaboration with the assembled disciples, it ought to work.

Problems of language

Debates about language and the lectionary come in two forms: issues relating to gender-exclusive language, a problem only for *RL*;[11] and the endless debate on 'which is the best translation?'

If one leaves aside arguments based on the aesthetic appeal of the Authorized Version (and related cultural arguments as exemplified by a bumper sticker I saw once in the US: 'If it ain't King James, it ain't Bible'), there are legitimate debates about which is the most suitable both for liturgy in general and for liturgy in particular situations and for particular groups. My own opening position is that asking 'which is best?' is an incomplete question, and so all answers offered are consequently incomplete – and so the argument goes round and round. Every translation is made with a particular purpose in mind, and it is a phenomenon of human language that one can, in any single rendering, only partially translate. Hence, translations are complementary rather than competing. So the question should be asked in this form: which is the best translation for this particular purpose or situation?

But before looking at how different versions might be used in the liturgy, we should consider a more fundamental problem. The Gospels

---

[10] Rothenbuhler 1998, 126.

[11] By the time *RCL* and *CWL* appeared this was a live issue and the use of gender-inclusive versions was taken for granted.

were composed in the light of 'the Scriptures' – that is the obvious bit – but what is often forgotten is that they were composed with the Greek translation of those Scriptures, commonly called 'the Septuagint', as the working text. It is not infrequent, however, that when we read a Gospel and its *related* first reading (and this happens more often than not in *RCL* and *CWL*, and almost invariably in *RL*) the two texts do not seem to gel nearly so clearly as the evangelist supposed. The explanation is obvious: all modern translations of the Old Testament are made directly from the Hebrew, but the Septuagint is a rather free translation at the best of times, and quite often a paraphrase, and it was this that lies behind the Gospels (see Figure 4).

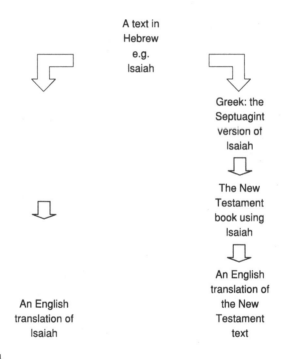

Figure 4

This is a simplified version of the sequences of translations by which an ancient text comes to us in our Bibles. It has to be described as 'simplified' because we have only limited certainty about the exact form of the Hebrew text that underlies the Septuagint, and the same applies to the form of the Septuagint underlying the Gospels, and the Gospel texts themselves result from editorial work both ancient and modern.

The problem has embarrassed Christians since the mid second century, and it still means what we often need in the liturgy is an Old Testament translation that does justice to the Septuagint – and thereby to the Gospel – rather than a standard one whose purpose is to reflect the Hebrew. There is no such translation readily available, so often adaptation, case by case, is the only way to bring out what is the memory lying behind the Gospel. In those cases where the Old Testament passage (given as the first reading) is quoted in the Gospel, then the simplest solution is to insert the translation of the evangelist's quote at the appropriate point. When it is a matter of allusion, or where the Gospel follows a blunder in the Septuagint, then the problem still needs to be addressed. It is worth remembering that despite having ever better editions of the Hebrew and the Septuagint, and increasingly with Aramaic paraphrases offering additional help, we often cannot be certain of the form of the biblical text being used by early Christian authors. This not only undermines appeals to verbal inerrancy with a contrary fact, but reminds us that often we have to proceed with the best approximation (> Koester 1989) – a fact we often miss when reading those telling footnotes in the NRSV: 'meaning of Gk uncertain' or 'other ancient authorities add'!

But what of the choices between existing translations? My approach is an application of the notion that no one translation fits all. If a preacher intends to examine a detail of a text in the homily, or carefully compare words and usages, then it is clearly necessary to have a text that permits that sort of examination, and de facto this now means the NRSV. If, however, the whole sweep of the story is what is needed, then one of the dynamic equivalent translations is usually better. One then picks the translation that matches the sense of a particular reading best – and I have often found, for example, that using the much-maligned Good News Bible for the Old Testament passage works well, with the often ignored Revised English Version for the letter, and then with the Jerusalem Bible for the Gospel. Similarly, when liturgy takes place in an informal setting – not a formal liturgical space – a very formal version seems somehow out of place; while in the solemn moments of the year somehow formal equivalence is needed. Moreover, since the 1980s, there have been special forms of *RL* available for use in liturgies with many children present.

A 'pick and mix' approach to translations has been employed in several Catholic liturgical books, subsequent to *RL*,[12] and was famously (or infamously) adopted in *ASB* (> Giles 2001, 229–30). However, I am not advocating that such a variety of translations be printed in a formal printing of the Lectionary – as such a practice would disrupt continuous reading and impose a translation strategy that will be as often inappropriate as not. Rather, it is good that there is a default translation – and that in turn suggests the NRSV as that translation – but we have to become more sensitive to the situation of the use of the Scriptures in an actual liturgical event. Situations will often occur in which the liturgy is enabled to communicate more effectively with an assembly when (following a balanced decision of pastoral needs: 'the version I like best' is not a liturgical criterion!) one opts for the use of another translation, and then this can be printed out for those who perform the readings from the many versions readily available electronically. Moreover, those who prepare resources for the liturgy should give this question consideration when preparing notes for particular Sundays and offer advice on whether one translation has marked advantages over another.

The second linguistic problem only concerns those who use *RL*. When *RL* appeared in 1969, many Catholics thought the whole issue of language had been solved: now the readings were to be in the daily language of the community, and that was that. By the time it was given a minor revision in 1982, the issue of sexist – i.e., non-inclusive – language had come on the scene but was not so high on the agenda that it was seen as a problem to continue using gendered language. Now after a further 30 years, it is a serious matter in Catholic worship (> Ramshaw 1988). Often when this question of inclusive language is raised, some people still simply dismiss it as a 'fad', and then argue that 'it is only a matter of words'. This defensive reaction is always annoying for two reasons: first, to dismiss the question as only 'a matter of words' forgets that we are there using words, words and more words to help us celebrate the revelation of God. To dismiss

---

[12] The 1973 English version of the Liturgy of the Hours ('the breviary') uses a variety of translations to very good effect; *RL* was initially produced in two identical editions, one with the RSV and one with the Jerusalem Bible, but when it was reissued in 1982 there was only one version: the Jerusalem Bible.

words so flippantly hides, one suspects, a belief that the whole Liturgy of the Word, which depends on words, is not really all that important after all. Second, for many people, and they are not only women, the use of non-inclusive language is deeply offensive and is a form of offence that they no longer have to endure in many aspects of life that have less reason to be sensitive to people's sense of self-worth than the liturgy. The simple fact is that Catholics have a problem that at the moment is officially thought not to exist: if ancient texts use non-inclusive language, then so must we! Yet every time a passage is read that contains obviously gender-exclusive language, there will be some people listening who will be upset and will have been alienated rather than helped by what they have heard.

What can be done about this? There have been several statements about the issue where various bishops have argued that even if there were to be a new Lectionary, changing to inclusive language would not be allowed as this would not be 'faithful to the Latin' or 'original'. Whether or not such arguments have any validity is not my concern here, but the prognosis is not good for an official inclusive-language edition any time soon. However, some communities, or individual readers who are offended by having to read what they consider sexist language, have come up with 'work arounds' such as printing out the passage from another translation (e.g. the NRSV) while invoking the canonical maxim: *cura animarum lex suprema* ('the care of souls is the supreme law'). And, of course, there are readers who whenever they meet sexist language simply alter the offending words without comment. This is a serious issue: it is a matter that should be discussed openly when readers meet, it should be addressed each week by liturgy planning groups, and then one of the simple remedies adopted.

As with the basic issues of lectionary design (structure, arrangement and size), so with these questions of translations and language, there is inherent need for compromise. We read texts in our language that were composed and used in a variety of languages (mainly Hebrew and Greek) and that themselves evolved in situations where the tradition's earlier texts were now only accessible through being texts heard in translations and paraphrases. We too then inherit these texts with the encrustations of long use and habits (some good, some bad) of long usage. And the language in which we now hear them is a living world language with multiple registers and dialects – we are often separated by a common language – and we are faced with two alternatives: either a tightly bonded community starts from scratch and creates its own translation just for itself, or, noting that that is not an option, we accept the necessary compromise of our situation, and proceed to use the Lectionary with good grace. However, there is always room for diligent pastors to tweak the language so as to make the message more effective in their particular situation.

Problems relating to the content of the Lectionary

When the Lectionary's content is discussed there are certain issues that are almost certain to come up – but not necessarily from the same people. The first, and most common, is that some of the readings – particularly those chosen for the second readings – are so badly formed as to be little more than poster-length slogans from Paul's letters. The problem is particularly noticeable in *RL* where there was a greater willingness to omit verses than is found in *RCL*; a willingness to begin and end readings without close attention to the natural textual units in the text; and a tendency to continue with very short – often just one or two verses – readings from Paul because that was the style of the epistle readings in the Tridentine Missal. The overall effect is that sometimes the second reading is short, but the audience is dropped into the middle of an argument and given a few staccato remarks (similar to those one can find as 'verse for the day' in pious diaries). Here is a clear case for future revisers of *RL* to learn from *RCL* and adopt its solutions. Not only does *RCL*'s arrangement of the second reading make more sense of the notion of continuous readings from the epistles, but the reading for any particular day is more likely to make sense. Interestingly, when *RCL* departs from *RL*, *CWL* usually tries to find a middle position or offer an option; however, in the matter of second readings where *RCL* most consistently differs from *RL*, *CWL* follows *RCL* without any nod in the *RL*'s direction.

A problem that is raised by those with a deeper sense of the value of the Old Testament is that the Lectionary's use of passages often leads to a problem of broken narratives. We do not get a whole story, but only an isolated element – and this, they argue, does not do justice to the original text. This is a problem to which there is no simple answer: the Lectionary is built on the core structure of its readings from the Gospels on the basis that it is the Gospel that must be heard at the gathering of the disciples. The Old Testament reading is then placed in a background or supporting role – and, consequently, given the time available, its narratives are broken up. When *RL* was designed, while it wanted to locate the Gospel within a history of salvation, it did not equate that with a survey of 'Bible history' nor, since it was linking particular passages from the Old Testament to the sequence of Gospels, did it see it as valuable to present Old Testament narratives in extended form. Moreover, from *RL*'s perspective, this was going to be accomplished in the two-year weekday cycle[13] – as, indeed, it has – but these readings are heard by very few people and, moreover, usually heard without the explanatory comment. Given the empirical reality that most people will encounter the formal proclamation of the Scriptures just once a week, at the principal gathering on Sunday, then those narratives have to be heard there or they will not be heard at all. It was with this problem in mind that *RCL* opted for its strategy for the use of the Old Testament between Pentecost and Advent (> Appendix 5), and while this does try to create a framework to enunciate the broad Old Testament narratives, it puts even more material into an already full Liturgy of the Word – without perhaps sufficient space to do so many *distinct* readings justice. We shall return to this issue in the next chapter.

When *RL* was being planned there were those who argued that if there was going to be a year for each of the first three evangelists, then there should be one for John also – so a four-year cycle (> Bugnini 1990, 417–18). The argument keeps resurfacing – though, anecdotally, I notice that it comes up at meetings of liturgists and among Scripture scholars, while I have never heard it raised at meetings of clergy or 'ordinary' Christians – and sometimes takes the form of an 'optional' four-year cycle or an 'optional' fourth year that could replace a year of the present three-year cycle. I have, I must admit, only limited patience with this appeal for 'the witness of John' for these reasons:

- The argument is really part of a desire to have everything included, but this is an argument from notional ideals rather than from the practicalities of action – and liturgy is activity. If compromise is

---

[13] Many of the narratives are also found in the Lectionary to the Office of Readings of the Liturgy of the Hours.

inevitable, then one must accept that the best is often the enemy of the good.

- The present three-year cycle still has not embedded itself in the con-sciousness of the churches that use it, and the Lectionary is still under-appreciated – and further changing will just destroy good work already done and add further complexity to the challenge of using any lectionary.

- There is already as much of John's Gospel read as there is of the Gospel of Luke (> Giles 2001, 231); and hearing some of John every year acts as an element of continuity.

- A new Johannine cycle would not add any more John to the 'amount' read, but make what is read from John to be heard less frequently.

- To imagine that the witness of John – used mainly as alternative perspectives within the seasons – is not heard is to conflate the presence of his voice with the number of verses used. The task is to note the distinctiveness of the Johannine voice when it is used rather than just see it as another variant of a harmonized single Gospel. So, for example, does one have a 'Christmas story homily' if one reads the Johannine prologue on Christmas day (> O'Loughlin 2009a)?

- The Gospels that are chosen from John are the ones that are com-monly most feared by preachers – and this sense of apprehension will not be removed by simply adding further passages.

- Adding a fourth 'optional' cycle would destroy the logic of cycles and make it simply a free-for-all; moreover, with that amount of choice, the Lectionary's basic planning shape would become redundant.

- At any gathering of those involved in the liturgy one hears of many problems with the Liturgy of the Word; while those who call for a 'Year of John' are, more often than not, removed from that level of liturgical involvement.

- If any change took place, it should have widespread agreement as there have been real benefits from having so many churches adopt the Lectionary: what odds would one get on a bet that one could make this rather specialized change and keep the current level of agreement?

7

The place of the Old Testament in the celebration of the New Covenant

No problem regarding the Lectionary is raised more frequently than a related set of questions about the place of the Old Testament within it. The questions come in three forms:

- Why bother with it at all? – the most frequent question;
- How does it relate to the rest of the readings?
- Why do we not use it as a basic text within the liturgy? – the least frequent question.

Despite their different forms, these questions are, in fact, closely related, and in this chapter I shall sketch out a view of the Old Testament in relation to the community of the New Covenant – particularly as it assembles as a local church – which I hope will provide *some* answers to all three questions. It is not possible to give a fully satisfactory answer because there are basic unresolved issues regarding the place of the Old Testament within Christian theology, and all that can be done here is to point them out.

The Scriptures of the disciples of Jesus

In the immediate aftermath of the Pentecost story in Acts we have Luke's image of what a perfect proclamation of the gospel looks like: Peter leading his audience through a series of scriptural (what we would now call: 'Old Testament') examples until the point that he can declare that 'God has made him both Lord and Messiah, this Jesus whom you crucified' (Acts 2.36 NRSV). This is not some historical memory of an actual speech preserved by Luke, but the product of his own profound reflection on the nature of being an evangelist. It is Luke's ideal presentation of the dynamic of announcing Jesus; and as we have already observed (> Chapter 1) the basis for that proclamation is the collective memory of Israel, a memory exemplified and codified in the books known collectively as 'the Scriptures'. Put another way, if one counts the various quotations and allusions to the Old Testament found in the New Testament one gets a figure close to 4,300.[1] In short, the new relationship – whose announcement we hear in the Gospels – only made sense to those who saw it as being built on the existing covenant. Therefore, if we are to appreciate our 'new' texts, then we have to have absorbed the content, the memory which gave them the shape they have.

We state formally in the Nicene Creed that Jesus rose on the third day 'in accordance with the scriptures' echoing 1 Corinthians 15.4, without realizing the implication that unless someone has an historical framework for belief, and so an historical sense of their own religious identity, then Christian faith can easily become the religious wrapping paper for Jesus as a good man or a religious philosopher. So what is that historical framework like? Its exact shape cannot be pinned down because it varied with times and groups of people (for example, at the time of Jesus alone we have Pharisees, Sadducees, Qumran, Zealots, Alexandrians, other Greek-speaking Jews, Essenes, followers of John, and many others); indeed, there were so many variations that many prefer to speak of 'ancient Judaisms' rather than of a monolithic 'Judaism' – and this variety continued to be reflected in those who followed the new Jesus-movement. However, there were certain constant elements. God was the creator of all, the instigator of history and its lord: this was seen in the ever popular stories from Genesis, often recalled in the psalms and then echoed in other writings found in our Old Testament. Then there is the moment of God choosing a people as his own – the events linked to Abraham. Then there are the great events linked with Moses: giving the law, deliverance from Egypt, the wanderings for forty years, the law and cult, and then the entry into the promised land. Then there is the division of the land and the arrival of kingship, followed by the building of the Temple. Then there were the prophets and the renewals of the covenant; as God sustained, defended and

---

[1] This is based on counting the list of references and allusions found in Nestle-Aland's edition of the New Testament – one should not attempt to be too precise as that list is a record of the clear allusions, and many would argue for far more cases where the New Testament can only be understood with reference to the Old.

even chastised his people. History was the story of a relationship, a covenant – the older term for this was 'testament' – between God and his people: 'I will take you as my people, and I will be your God' (Exod. 6.7). And, perhaps most significantly from our perspective today: history was legible.

Hearing about the past told one about God, the community to which one belonged, and established one's religious context. Moreover, for many, and this would include most of those who placed their faith in Jesus, this history was a way of looking forwards into the future and to a time of a still more perfect relationship that was going to come about. Then at that future moment, through his loving action, the Lord would send his 'anointed one', his 'christ', his 'messiah' – they are interchangeable terms – who would gather together the scattered people and lead this renewed Israel as its victorious king. For some, such as John the Baptist, this 'day of the Lord' was going to be a day of reckoning and judgement. For others, it was to be the time of deliverance whose image would be that of the day of a great banquet, the foretaste of the heavenly banquet (> Smith 1991), and it appears that this was a view shared by Jesus himself (> Meier 1994, 964–6). It is the totality of that memory and identity that we encounter in the collection of texts we refer to as 'the Old Testament' – or to be more precise: in those writings reflecting the Older Covenant.

Once the gospel was being preached beyond the people of Israel, the followers of Jesus were presented with a basic problem, which remains with us to this day, in two parts: first, how could people who did not already belong to the Older Covenant make its history their own, and second, how could they absorb that past as their vision of the history of the world and thereby make sense of Jesus? The answer to the first part of the question lay in seeing the covenant with one people as preparatory to a covenant that could extend to all peoples and to the ends of the earth. The answer to the second part of the problem was to read those Scriptures as the basis of history, and then for each people to integrate their own history within an overall framework derived from the Gospels. Thus the Church found itself committed to preaching and expounding its message under two headings: first, the story of the Christ ('the new covenant' eventually as recalled in the list (canon) of writings that became synonymous with it: 'the New Testament'), and second, the story of the earlier covenant – seen as preparatory for the New Covenant – which was identified with the Scriptures they had inherited, and which then became synonymous with that older relationship: 'the Old Testament'. And so the Church has been reading, imagining and expounding those texts as its own pre-history ever since – and it has seen this process as having a place in its liturgy: blessing the Father in union with his Christ, assumes that we approach the Father as one of his people and, therefore, out of the history of his covenant.

Lectionary strategies

This task presents us with certain challenges when it comes to the Lectionary and the actual use of the writings of the Older Covenant in the liturgy. The first problem is practical: how do we communicate that overall memory so that the community gathered to hear the gospel – and celebrate its covenant – can appreciate it in its larger context: the history of God's dealing with his people? This was tackled by *RL* by assuming that one provided the older texts piece by piece in so far as they related to a particular passage of the Gospels – and these Gospel passages were arranged according to the seasons and semi-continuous reading (> Chapter 5). In committing itself to this policy it abandoned any notion that the Sunday Lectionary (the Easter Vigil apart) could convey any summary framework of the Older Covenant such as that which underlies Peter's speech in Acts 2. *RCL*, while taking over this approach from *RL* for the seasons of Christmas and Easter, decided that it wanted to introduce a summary narrative sweep through the Scriptures of the Old Testament and so adopted the three cycles of readings – which are not related to the Gospel of the day – for Ordinary Time after Pentecost (> Appendix 5).

The advantages and disadvantages of each strategy cancel one another out almost completely. On the one hand, *RL*'s constant linking of Old Testament and Gospel readings allows a better appreciation of the particular Gospel, and gives the readings (Old Testament, Psalm, Gospel) a coherence, but it does not help create a collective memory of the overall 'framework' of the Older Covenant. On the other hand, *RCL* aids the development of that framework, and a general appreciation of the Older Covenant assists in a better overall appreciation of the new, but on any Sunday there are three unconnected reading cycles, and sometimes a Gospel needs its underlying

Old Testament passage if its significance is to be drawn out. (But we shall return to this comparison of the relative merits of *RL* and *RCL* in regard to the Old Testament later in this chapter.) *CWL* has an embarrassment of riches in that it offers both; but the community has to choose one or another strategy for a period of three years if the Lectionary planners' work – for either strategy, but especially for that of *RCL*[2] – is to bear fruit. However, while this overall perspective makes excellent sense, when we actually start linking the Old and New Testaments we find that there are more problems than answers.

The relationship of two covenants

But there is a less obvious challenge facing anyone who wants to link the Old Testament with the New: *how* are they related? The simplest solution to this issue (adopted both in the strategy for Ordinary Time after Pentecost in *RCL*, and in this book) is to look at the issue in terms of collective memory and our understanding of the Gospels: unless we know what was the memory of the first communities where the Gospels were preached, we cannot access their implicit significance. Then when we take a Gospel in its totality we can see it as one way in which an early preacher (Mark, Matthew, Luke or John) saw the hope of Israel being fulfilled in Jesus. Moreover, in many particular passages in the Lectionary it is relatively clear – especially if one makes allowance for the use of the Septuagint as the Scriptures of the first churches – to see how the Old underlies the New, is its background, and the key to its context: for example, one can only appreciate why Mark has a period of darkness at noon in his passion (15.33) if one knows that he sees this as fulfilling the prophecy in Amos 8.9–10, or why John has 'I thirst' (19.28) unless one recalls that John says, 'in order to fulfil the scripture' – when John probably had Psalm 69.21 in mind.

However, for most of Christian history a far more theologically grounded argument has been used: that the interrelationship of the

---

[2] Since the *RCL* strategy depends on the sweep of readings, it only bears fruit if one follows the cycle; the *RL* piecemeal approach focuses the Old Testament reading on that day's Gospel, and so it works Sunday by Sunday.

events narrated, and teaching, in the Old Testament are linked to the events and teaching in the New as part of the whole divine plan. We see this belief in those examples from two proclamations of the Passion: what happened was predicted and what was announced beforehand was now fulfilled. This belief in the intrinsic connection between the events of the two covenants pervades the Gospels, but is nowhere better expressed than in the Emmaus story in Luke: 'then beginning with Moses and all the prophets, [Jesus] interpreted to them the things about himself in all the scriptures' (24.27 NRSV). The whole of the Old made sense in terms of Jesus – indeed, only when one 'factored in Jesus' would they make full sense (> De Lubac 1959). It was on the foundation of this belief that was built the whole edifice of the Christian interpretation of the Scriptures until modern times. This view was reaffirmed by the Second Vatican Council in 1965 in these terms:

> The economy of the Old Testament was deliberately so oriented that it should prepare for and declare in prophecy the coming of Christ, redeemer of all men, and of the messianic kingdom (cf. Lk 24:44; Jn 5:39; 1 Pet 1:10), and should indicate it by means of different types (cf. 1 Cor 10:11). . . . Christians should accept with veneration these writings which give expression to a lively sense of God, which are a storehouse of sublime teaching on God and of sound wisdom on human life, as well as a wonderful treasury of prayers; in them, too, the mystery of our salvation is present in a hidden way.
>
> God, the inspirer and author of the books of both Testaments, in his wisdom has so brought it about that the New should be hidden in the Old and that the Old should be made manifest in the New.
>
> (*Dei Verbum* 15–16; > Flannery 1975, 759)

This quotation is not only a remarkably clear summary of an older approach to the Scriptures that is alien to many people, but makes explicit the rationale that underlies the whole approach to the Old Testament in the Lectionary. It is explicitly the case with *RL* (and those parts of *RCL* that follow it), and can be implied in those parts of *RCL* which are distinctive from *RL* (i.e., the unrelated Old Testament sequences in Ordinary Time).

What this means in practice is that the relationship of the Old Testament reading and the Gospel may be obvious – one the background of the other – but also that they may be related using the theological hermeneutic of typology and following rules of exegesis which we today, in fact, never use. Like it or not, when we today examine the Scriptures we do this within an historical hermeneutic which has no place for the older methods, which are seen as appealing to accommodations, reading anachronistically, and arguing in circles. The older method died not just because of the rise of a new style of exegesis, but because its 'results' could not withstand the body of historical evidence that contradicted its basic assumptions. But here is the dilemma: on many occasions – and this is more true of *RL* than *RCL* – there are many passages whose location in the Lectionary can only be understood by recalling that the selectors of those passages worked between 1964 and 1969 (> Bugnini 1990, 419–20) in a milieu which also produced *Dei Verbum* as a 'dogmatic constitution' (> Seasoltz 1980, 170–1) for the Catholic Church in November 1965.

This is a major difficulty that affects the selection of the Old Testament passage almost as often as not: and when either a preacher or someone else in the assembly says that they cannot 'see' the connection, they are being completely truthful. What one sees in any text is a function of the hermeneutic within which that text is given meaning. For most of us today, whether we are studying the Old Testament or not, such a hermeneutic as was used in the Lectionary is not part of our view of the world. Moreover, we cannot simply adopt it – though we may 'sympathize' with it when we try to understand how Christians in the past used such an understanding – because it was dissatisfaction with its inability to answer our questions that led to its abandonment. Every so often someone makes a call for this view of Scripture 'to be brought back' – as if one could bring back the bright snows of last winter – but anyone who tries this brings the whole endeavour of being an historical religion into disrepute.[3]

Regrettably, because of the use of this hermeneutic in the Lectionary – now foreign not just to most theological training in the use of the Scriptures but also to our culture – many faced with the passages from the Old Testament they find on Sunday just

---

[3] This notion that one can simply 'bring back' a hermeneutic that no longer belongs within our culture is, after all, but a variant of that older hermeneutic that animates biblical fundamentalists.

wonder how this could possibly have any value for understanding the Gospel. Looking at the two readings side by side does not produce enlightenment but exasperation! When this experience is then combined with a more general cultural suspicion about anything 'ancient' – especially when it is the 'old' in comparison to another ancient set of documents labelled 'new' – then frustration often leads to a complete failure to see any value in reading the Old Testament in the liturgy. The dated hermeneutic implicit in the selection of the passages works to undermine any appreciation that the Old Testament is of value to a Christian community today.

Implicit messages

Whenever an individual or a group looks at the world, or a body of information such as a text or a collection of texts, they employ a hermeneutic – a point of view, a perspective, an horizon – that shows up certain matters as important while it leaves others invisible in the background. It is these shifts in hermeneutic that generate the questions of 'how on earth could they have said that?' or 'how on earth were they so blind that they did not see that?' – and makes the past 'a foreign country' where they do things differently.[4]

One implicit message in the typology hermeneutic is that the 'Old Testament' does not really have an integrity of its own, but can only be properly read by those who possess the New. This was the notion that those who read it in light of the New possess the 'fuller meaning' (*sensus plenior*). This is the explicit claim that the Christian reader is the person for whom it was 'really' written – and as the ideal reader that person's interpretation is not only superior but 'the truth in its fullness' (> O'Loughlin 1998). However, implicit in this is the notion that the first covenant has run its course and that the Christians have replaced the Jews as the chosen people – in effect, the Jews are stuck in the past and they do not even really know what they take to be their own books. This is not only arrogant, but fails to do justice either to good theology or, more importantly, to that basic reverence that is aware that the infinity of God is not

---

[4] The image is from the opening lines of L. P. Hartley's 1953 novel, *The Go-Between*.

tied down in neat systems, and it is a notion that has long provoked anti-Jewish attitudes among Christians. This danger, that reading the Old Testament can easily degenerate into a simple narrative that 'we know it all' – and then be further developed into the notion that Judaism is in a religious 'cul-de-sac' – is something that we must all guard against (> Ramshaw 1990). It is a particular danger when the link between the Old Testament passage and the Gospel is made typologically, not only because this is open to binary explanations of 'imperfect–perfect'/ 'shadow–reality' styles of analysis where the first reading always comes off 'worse' by comparison with the Gospel, but because that style of exegesis has been a contributory factor to Christian anti-Jewish polemics from the second century until the twentieth.

Because of the dangers involved some have suggested that the terms 'Old Testament' and 'New Testament' should be dropped in favour of 'First Testament' and 'Second Testament'. But laudable as this suggestion is, it is not simply enough to change terminology (and I suspect that the other terms – for all their inaccuracy – are so firmly embedded that they would not disappear) because Christians will continue to use those Scriptures in making sense of their faith. What is needed is constant hermeneutical vigilance coupled with a willingness to point out in preaching the dangers of that approach whenever a community is likely to hear the combination of readings in an anti-Jewish way. That said, the problem would be mitigated if *RL* had not committed itself to a typological hermeneutic, but one of memory and context (> Sloyan 1989). So, to return to the comparison of the strategies of *RL* and *RCL* for the Old Testament: in so far as *RCL* sequences in Ordinary Time seek to promote a general awareness of the mindset within which the first preaching took place, as distinct from an implicit appeal to typology, its arrangement is to be preferred to *RL*. But once one asserts that, one should remember that it assumes that one avoids a 'supersessionist' hermeneutic (i.e., that the Church is the replacement of Israel in the divine plan), and also that people listening can follow three unrelated trains of thought from one Sunday to the next over a period of about five months (including the summer holidays) and then assemble those memories over three years into a greater whole! If the Lectionary as a whole makes demands on our communication skills and the retentiveness of its audience, the *RCL*'s sequences make massive demands on our attentiveness.

Who are we and what are we doing?

There is a tendency to begin discussion of the use of the Old Testament with the contents page of a book. The whole book is called 'The Bible' – a name which carries a vast range of cultural associations, many of them at variance with a theology of any church that gathers for the Eucharist – and then there are the two 'testaments'. A 'testament' (from the Latin *testamentum* translating the word *diathēkē* used by Paul, Luke and the author of Hebrews) is the word for the relationship that is established by the Christ between us his people and the Father. So in accounts of the Eucharist in Paul (1 Cor. 11.25) and Luke (22.20) Jesus refers to the new relationship that is established in his blood between those who share in his cup, and the Father. But as commonly used 'testament' is the name of a subdivision of the book: the new and old collections of books. But to constantly say 'the books of the Old Testament' or 'the books of the New Testament' seems too wordy, while 'the books of the Older Relationship' or 'the books of the second Relationship' invites the sneer: 'Why can't you just call it what we have always called it?' Then we get into books and for each of them we have preconceived ideas: 'Genesis' – simply wrong, it did not happen that way; Exodus – deserts; 'Leviticus' – boring stuff about blood; 'Jeremiah' – giving out about something; 'Wisdom' – which one, there seem to be several of them? 'Qoheleth' – never heard of it! 'Maccabees' – should that really be in the Bible?

A far better starting point is to ask who we are: we are the people of the covenant established by Jesus whom we confess as Lord and Christ – and gather as a church to express this relationship in the meal of blessing and thanking the Father. This testament calls on us to recall the events that established it – the paschal mystery of the life, death and resurrection of Jesus. And that mystery can only be understood in terms of the covenant that God had already established with his people and which was celebrated in their Scriptures. So just as our covenant is located within another covenant – so the books of that testament have to be adopted by us. It is the challenge of expounding Christian faith to convey this overall perspective; it is the challenge of preaching to locate the passage from the Gospel on a specific day, within an actual community, within that overall vision.

Additional note: the use of the Psalms

Despite the fact that many of the Psalms had a place in the Temple liturgy and have been used by Christians in their gatherings since the earliest days (> Eph. 5.19; Col. 3.16) they have not figured significantly in this book. This neglect is due to the different manner in which congregations use the psalter in comparison with how they hear the readings. First, while the readings are performed for the community to hear them, the psalm is more akin to the group singing, except that the material has a biblical source. Because of this difference in how we approach them, the psalm is best treated as part of a discussion of the place of music in the liturgy.

It is sufficient here to note that:

- The selection of the psalms does not follow any systematic pattern within the psalter; rather each is chosen as, normally, somehow linked to the first reading, and is presented as a meditative reflection on that reading. So, in effect, the same psalm can be used with many different texts. On occasions, the choice of psalm is based on a verse from that psalm being used in the Gospel, and on these occasions it functions more closely with other Old Testament readings.

- Because the psalm is envisaged as being sung – and this can take so many forms depending on the musical tradition and resources of a local church – it is an unstable element in the Liturgy of the Word. Not only can it take many forms. A psalm can be read responsorially one week, antiphonally another, or by a solo voice; sung straight through as a congregational piece (e.g. 'The Lord is my Shepherd' to the tune 'Crimond'), or as a choir piece, or following the older form of the gradual, or as a Taizé chant – the list of variations is almost endless. Likewise, a psalm is the item most likely to be replaced by another psalm, canticle, hymn, or with another musical element, or even dispensed with when not sung. Therefore, trying to plan for it as part of a strategy for using the Lectionary, in the way one can plan for the other elements in the Liturgy of the Word, is impossible.

- The psalms, despite constant use for two millennia by Christians, can pose all the issues relating to the use of the Old Testament in a focused form. For instance, does one use them as ancient religious poetry (the default position in most congregations today) or as prayers uttered in Christ or with Christ or about Christ (which is the traditional, typological interpretation animating their use not just in the eucharistic liturgy but in all liturgy)? Here the whole question of one's hermeneutic of the Old Testament can come to rest on a single verse! Take this example from Psalm 51.11 (NRSV): 'Do not cast me away from your presence, and do not take your holy spirit from me.'[5] Most today read this reference to 'holy spirit' as a reference to the divine presence, but for most of Christian history it was read as 'the Holy Spirit', whose full identity was not yet known.

Therefore, as a liturgical element it is best to treat the psalm under the heading of 'music'[6] rather than 'lectionary'; but as a piece of our scriptural inheritance – a necessary memory for us due to the place they held in forming the imaginations of Jesus and his disciples – they should be treated in a similar manner to the rest of the Scriptures of the first covenant.

---

[5] *RL* uses this translation: 'do not cast me away from your presence, nor deprive me of your holy spirit' (The Grail).

[6] The same can be said about the greeting before the Gospel and, in the case of *RL*, for the few 'sequences' (e.g. *Veni, sancte Spiritus* at Pentecost) that are still used. While these can be valuable additions to the liturgy, a satisfactory treatment would be out of place in a short introduction focused on the Lectionary.

8

Towards the future

This book has attempted to impart an appreciation of the Lectionary while at the same time making clear both the challenges it presents to all who use it, and its problems. A lectionary such as we have now, planned on a grand scale, which has to accommodate the reading of the Scriptures on the largest feasible scale, with the demands of celebrating the Christian year, is a novelty in the history of Christianity. It has been around for barely a half-century – a short time in terms of the lifespan of liturgical books – and we have only begun to learn of its possibilities. Like every human work it is imperfect; and given the nature of lectionaries as acts of balancing various demands, there will always be temptation to stress another aspect of the equation and suggest it as an improvement. Over the years I have heard and read of many suggestions for this or that improvement, and indeed made such suggestions myself, but while there is always room for some minor adjustments, I do not consider that this is a time for a new lectionary or even a major revision. The more one would revise, the stronger the case for a complete 'start over': but such would just create a different set of problems from those we have now – the Scriptures in all their varieties and with the problems attending them and their liturgical use would still be there – and it would destroy the de facto harmony between so many churches, over a crucial element of liturgy that emerged after the publication of *RL*. Often the hardest decision that confronts one when contemplating improvements is to know 'when to leave "well enough" alone'!

However, that does not mean that there are not ways by which the existing Lectionary – remembering that a lectionary is a structure and list of scriptural references before it is a book – cannot be made more accessible, or its contents more amenable to effective com-munication and celebration as part of a community's liturgy. Likewise, by keeping in mind the whole structure's shortcomings one can com-pensate for them in actual practice.

111

For the vast majority of Christians the event of a gathering is a moment in a series of similar moments, and no more. This is the attitude we adopt when we go shopping: I go out for my shopping today, tomorrow I shall need to go shopping again and so will be back in the same shop probably buying many of the same articles. So we gather to bless the Father today, and next Sunday will do so again – it is, in a phrase one still hears from Catholics, the habit of 'getting Mass on Sundays' – and on each occasion you 'get' some Scripture and a sermon. However, this approach is worse than useless when it comes to an appreciation of the Lectionary: it is celebrating seasons (in the seasons) made up of distinct elements – the various feasts; and it is celebrating different presentations of the mystery of Jesus outside the seasons. One must therefore think of it as more like the lectures that make up a module, or the instalments of a series. In order to present its larger agenda the Lectionary had to take a form that is at variance with much human expectation about 'going to church' – and this is a major weakness. However, bearing this in mind, one can then convey the larger vision of the overall plan in preaching and catechesis: the Lectionary is not just there, it must be explained to be appreciated.

It is a natural human tendency to seek links between various parts of any event: the balloons, the cake, the presents and the singing of 'Happy birthday' are all connected elements of a birthday party. If we go to a committee meeting we expect all the papers to somehow relate to the pressing business of the day and we tend to link the various issues together, and we praise 'joined up thinking'. When it comes to the readings we are no different: we hear the New Testament letter after the Old Testament reading and make comparisons and links in our mind; then we add the Gospel to that process. Indeed, many people just cannot separate the readings into different streams, while liturgists often argue that such a link is a basic expectation that should be fulfilled (> Ramshaw 1990) – and many preachers cannot resist finding links also! However, the Lectionary is far more complex – for good reason – and we need to keep that complexity in mind. We can summarize it thus: in Advent-Christmastide and Lent-Eastertide the Lectionary is determined by the season and the day, therefore, there is a link between all three readings. For the rest of the year the principle of semi-continuous reading applies, such that the Gospel and the second readings are not connected (except by coincidence) but run in separate cycles. In *RL* the Gospel cycle determines the Old Testament, while in *RCL* there is for 24 Sundays each year a third independent cycle.

While a thematic coherence might please many, the liturgy sees 'themes' as exceptions; but the very fact of remembering that the plan is there to serve other purposes than a perceived coherence on a Sunday helps eliminate confusion and the sense of bafflement which is alienating.

Another characteristic of humans is that we love understanding patterns and systems – the internal logic of complex form fascinates and attracts us – and we only have to look at the number of people who find Sudoku addictive to see this. By contrast, nothing is so off-putting as the sense of jumble, chaos and randomness. One of the great strengths of the Lectionary is that it manifests conscious, deliberative and careful planning, and so one can provide a rationale (even if one might not accept that rationale when it is typological, as it always is in the seasons) for why a passage is being read on a particular day. Here is a paradox: the complexity of its planning over a three-year cycle seems off-putting; however, once its rationale is comprehended, it has the effect of increasing the value of the reading on any particular Sunday because the sense that that reading is just 'what happens to be on' is removed. The appreciation of each part is increased in direct proportion to any increase in appreciation of the Lectionary's big ideas. The converse also holds true: those who dismiss the Lectionary – apart from those who are ideologically opposed to lectionaries – usually have least awareness of its planning, and how that planning can facilitate a greater overall understanding of the Gospels.

The Lectionary (*RL* always and *RCL* to a lesser extent) adopts a typological hermeneutic with regard to the Old Testament. This is problematic in many ways and – since it never really worked but always required ever more accommodations – is a fundamental weakness of the Lectionary. Moreover, it carries with it the danger that it can lead to a very dangerous view of Judaism and of Judaism in relationship to Christianity. We have to approach the Lectionary conscious of these problems – they can make opaque the reasoning by which an Old Testament passage is chosen, and encourage a tendency to compare the two religions in the manner of a modern advertising campaign: the bright, new, improved formula versus the dowdy old formula of yesterday. Only constant vigilance can avoid such caricatures and theological silliness; and being aware of the problem should also make us alert to recognize how, without that seeking to appropriate the memory that was present in those who first confessed Jesus as Lord, we shall leave ourselves blind to much of the gospel.

Having noted the need to share in the memory of the first disciples we have to be aware of the problems of language in lectionaries and keep them continually before us as we prepare for the liturgy.

First, the issue of inclusive language: this need will evolve with time and vary from culture to culture; we must ensure that no one hearing the gospel hears it in an alienating form.

Second, we must keep in mind that there is no ideal translation, but various ways and styles of translating that are suited to particular tasks or groups. When it comes to translations I always recall a poster in a butcher's shop where my mother bought meat. It read, and showed pictures of 'one joint of beef – twenty ways to cook it'. So with translations: each brings out something that may suit an occasion or be out of place in a situation. Picking a translation is a practical matter with many contributing factors – and it is a weakness that the Lectionary when printed as a book comes in just one flavour.

Third, often the link between the Gospel and an Old Testament passage turns on the latter's form in the Septuagint, as can be seen in the margins of a Greek New Testament. Unfortunately, by going for fixed translations of the Old Testament – invariably made from Hebrew without reference to the Septuagint – in printed lectionaries these links are often hidden. We should bear in mind the complexity of our religious history while remembering that the status of the Lectionary rests in its selection of passages, not in the translations chosen for the printed object called 'the Lectionary'.

Next Sunday when the reader opens the book – with greater or lesser formality depending on the tradition – one thing will be certain: the reader will read the passage aloud yet most of the reader's audience will also be able to read, have texts of their own in their hands, and indeed may be reading the passage for themselves. This is deeply ironical, for not only is it simply unnecessary to go to such trouble, it also brings individualism into a collective act of worship, and it subjects aural texts – whose origins we claim to honour – to the treatment more appropriate to scholastic texts. We must remember that the reading of the Scriptures in the assembled community, gathered in Christ, is the performance of our memory and an enactment of the kerygma: in this community listening we are not engaged in Scripture study but seeking to be attentive to the Spirit. But the sad fact is that most will keep on wanting to have their own piece of paper to read in silence, and thereby engage in worship as if it were simply a common 'service-point' for acquiring individuals' needs. In such a situation we should be slow to project onto the Lectionary, by way of criticism or suggestions for improvement, the demands of our own limited culture.

Finally, what the late Bishop Kenneth Stevenson said at the end of his 1998 introduction to *CWL* is true of all the various forms of the modern lectionary family, and succinctly summarizes the challenges facing every community who uses it:

> No lectionary is perfect, and every lectionary necessarily has something provisional about it . . . But this particular scheme . . . will, it is hoped, nourish and sustain the people of God in their eucharistic worship for many years to come. The fruit of ecumenical collaboration, biblical as well as liturgical, it can claim to be a significant landmark in the Church catholic's attention to what the Spirit has to say to us as we gather around the Lord's Table.

Appendix 1

The sequence of readings for Advent and Christmastide

For each Sunday or feast,

- the readings on the first line are from *RL*;
- where *RCL* differs from *RL*, its readings are placed in **bold** on the line beneath;
- where *CWL* differs from either *RL* or *RCL*, its readings are placed on the second or third line in *italics*;
- where *CWL* follows *RCL*, against *RL*, the reference is placed in ***bold italics***;
- optional sections or additions to readings are placed in [ ];
- readings given as alternatives are placed in { };
- in those cases where all three Lectionaries are identical in noting an optional 'shorter form', this has been ignored in this table;
- other combinations are noted *in situ*.

For example, the Gospel on the Fourth Sunday of Advent in *RCL*, followed by *CWL*, is Matthew 1.18–25 which is Matthew's textual unit, but in *RL* the final verse is omitted; this difference between the Lectionaries is expressed thus:

Matt. 1.18–24
Matt. 1.18–25

Table A1.1 Year A: 'The year of Matthew'

Sunday – feast	First reading	Second reading	Gospel
1 Advent	Isa. 2.1–5	Rom. 13.11–14	Matt. 24.37–44 *Matt. 24.36–44*
2 Advent	Isa. 11.1–10	Rom. 15.4–9 *Rom. 15.4–13*	Matt. 3.1–12
3 Advent	Isa. 35.1–16, 10 *Isa. 35.1–10*	Jas. 5.7–10	Matt. 11.2–11
4 Advent	Isa. 7.10–14 *Isa. 7.10–16*	Rom. 1.1–7	Matt. 1.18–24 *Matt. 1.18–25*
Christmas Eve	Isa. 62.1–5 **RCL** omits *2 Sam. 7.1–5,* *8–11, 16*	Acts 13.16–17, 22–25 – *Acts 13.16–26*	Matt. 1.1–25 – *Luke 1.67–79*
Christmas Midnight* / Set 1	Isa. 9.1–7 *Isa. 9.2–7*	Titus 2.11–14	Luke 2.1–14 *[with vv. 15–20]*
Christmas Dawn* / Set 2	Isa. 62.11–12 *Isa. 62.6–12*	Titus 3.4–7	Luke 2.15–20 *Luke 2.[1–7,] 8–20*
Christmas Daytime* / Set 3	Isa. 52.7–10	Heb. 1.1–6 *Heb. 1.1–4,* *[5–12]*	John 1.1–18 *John 1.1–14*
Holy Family / 1 AC	Ecclus. 3.2–6, 12–14 *Isa. 63.7–9*	Col. 3.12–21 *Heb. 2.10–18*	Matt. 2.13–15, 19–23 Matt. 2.13–23 *Matt. 2.13–26*
1 Jan. Mary, Mother of God / **Holy Name of Jesus** / *Naming and Circumcision of Jesus*	Num. 6.22–27	Gal. 4.4–7	Luke 2.16–21 *Luke 2.15–21*
1 Jan. **New Year's Day**	Eccles. 3.1–13	Rev. 21.1–6a	Matt. 25.31–46
2 AC	Ecclus. 24.1–2, 8–12 *Jer. 31.7–14* {Ecclus. 24.1–12}	Eph. 1.3–6, 15–18 *Eph. 1.3–14*	John 1.1–18 *John 1.[1–9,]* *10–18*
Epiphany	Isa. 60.1–6	Eph. 3.2–3, 5–6 *Eph. 3.1–12*	Matt. 2.1–12

* The three sets of readings are laid out in *RL* under a traditional formula that made an assumption that many taking part in the liturgy would be present at several, or all, of the celebrations. This clearly had serious pastoral implications since most people only attend the Eucharist once and expect to hear the Christmas story. Hence a new rubric was added in *RL* (1982). 'In Masses celebrated on Christmas Day, the readings given below are used, with the option of choosing more appropriate readings from any one of the three Masses according to the pastoral needs of each celebration' (> O'Loughlin 2006, 174–7). *RCL* and *CWL* took the simpler, and wiser, course of presenting them as alternative 'sets' of readings.

Table A1.2 Year B: 'The year of Mark'

Sunday – Feast	First reading	Second reading	Gospel
1 Advent	Isa. 63.16–17; 64.1, 3–8 *Isa. 64.1–9*	1 Cor. 1.3–9	Mark 13.33–37 *Mark 13.24–37*
2 Advent	Isa. 40.1–5, 9–11 *Isa. 40.1–11*	2 Pet. 3.8–14 *2 Pet. 3.8–15a*	Mark 1.1–8
3 Advent	Isa. 61.1–2, 10–11 *Isa. 61.1–4, 8–11*	1 Thess. 5.16–24	John 1.6–8, 19–28
4 Advent	2 Sam. 7.1–5, 8–11, 16 *2 Sam. 7.1–11, 16*	Rom. 16.25–27	Luke 1.26–38
Christmas Eve Christmas Midnight / Set 1 Christmas Dawn / Set 2 Christmas Daytime / Set 3	As Year A		
Holy Family / 1 AC	Gen. 15.1–6; 21.1–3 *Isa. 61.10—62.3*	Heb. 11.8, 11–12, 17–19 *Gal. 4.4–7*	Luke 2.22–40 *Luke 2.15–21*
1 Jan. all options	As Year A		
2 AC	As Year A		
Epiphany	As Year A		

Table A1.3 Year C: 'The year of Luke'

Sunday – Feast	First reading	Second reading	Gospel
1 Advent	Jer. 33.14–16	1 Thess. 3.12—4.2 *1 Thess. 3.9–13*	Luke 21.25–28, 34–36 *Luke 21.25–36*
2 Advent	Baruch 5.1–9 **Mal. 3.1–4** *CWL offers* *both as options*	Phil. 1.3–6, 8–11 *Phil 1.3–11*	Luke 3.1–6
3 Advent	Zeph. 3.14–18 *Zeph. 3.14–20*	Phil. 4.4–7	Luke 3.10–18 *Luke 3.7–18*
4 Advent	Mic. 5.1–4 *Mic. 5.2–5a*	Heb. 10.5–10	Luke 1.39–44 *Luke 1.39–45,* *[46–55]*
Christmas Eve Christmas Midnight / Set 1 Christmas Dawn / Set 2 Christmas Daytime / Set 3	As Year A		
Holy Family / 1 AC	1 Sam. 1.20–22, 24–28 *1 Sam. 2.18–20, 26*	1 John 3.1–2, 21–24 *Col. 3.12–17*	Luke 2.41–52
1 Jan. all options	As Year A		
2 AC	As Year A		
Epiphany	As Year A		

Appendix 2

The sequence of readings for
Lent and Eastertide

See Appendix 1 for a guide to codes used here.

Year A: 'The year of Matthew'

Table A2.1 Year A: Readings for Lent and Eastertide

Sunday – Feast	First reading	Second reading	Gospel
Ash Wednesday	Joel 2.12–18 *Joel 2.1–2, 12–17* *{Isa. 58.1–12}*	2 Cor. 5.20—6.2 *2 Cor. 5.20—6.10*	Matt. 6.1–6, 16–18 *Matt. 6.1–6,* *16–21* *{John 8.2–11}*
1 Lent	Gen. 2.7–9, 3.1–7 *Gen. 2.15–17, 3.1–7*	Rom. 5.12–19	Matt. 4.1–11
2 Lent	Gen. 12.1–4	2 Tim. 1.8–10 *Rom. 4.1–5, 13–17*	Matt. 17.1–9 *John 3.1–17*
3 Lent	Exod. 17.3–7 *Exod. 17.1–7*	Rom. 5.1–2, 5–8 *Rom. 5.1–11*	John 4.5–42
4 Lent	1 Sam. 16.1, 6–7, 10–13 *1 Sam. 16.1–13*	Eph. 5.8–14	John 9.1–41
Mothering *Sunday [option]*	*Exod. 2.1–10 or* *1 Sam. 1.20–28*	*2 Cor. 1.3–7 or* *Col. 3.12–17*	*Luke 2.33–35 or* *John 19.25b–27*
5 Lent	Ezek. 37.12–14 *Ezek. 37.1–14*	Rom. 8.8–11 *Rom. 6.6–11*	John 11.1–45
Palm Sunday	– Isa. 50.4–7 *Isa. 50.4–9a*	– Phil. 2.6–11 *Phil. 2.5–11*	Matt. 21.1–11* Matt. 26.14—27.66
Monday	Isa. 42.1–7 *Isa. 42.1–9*	– *Heb. 9.11–15*	John 12.1–11
Tuesday	Isa. 49.1–6 *Isa. 49.1–7*	– *1 Cor. 1.18–31*	John 13.21–33, 36–38 *John 12.20–36*
Wednesday	Isa. 50.4–9	– *Heb. 12.1–3*	Matt. 26.14–25 *John 13.21–32*

---

* Gospel for use before the Procession with the Palms/*Liturgy of the Palms*: all three Lectionaries are identical.

Table A2.1 (continued)

Sunday – Feast	First reading	Second reading	Gospel
Maundy Thursday	Exod. 12.1–8, 11–14 *Exod. 12.1–4, [5–10,] 11–14*	1 Cor. 11.23–26	John 13.1–15 *John 13.1–17, 31b–35*
Good Friday	Isa. 52.13—53.12	Heb. 4.14–16; 5.7–9 *{Heb. 10.16–25}*	John 18.1—19.42
Easter Eve	*Job 14.1–14 or Lam. 3.1–9, 19–24*	*1 Pet. 4.1–8*	*Matt. 27.57–66 or John 19.38–42*
Easter Vigil	**See Table A2.2**	Rom. 6.3–11	Matt. 28.1–10
Easter Day	Acts 10.34, 37–43 *Acts 10.34–43 {Jer. 31.1–6}*	Col. 3.1–4 *{1 Cor. 5.6–8} {Acts 10.34–43}*	John 20.1–9 (or any of the vigil gospels) On the evening of Easter day: Luke 24.13–35 *John 20.1–18 {Matt. 28.1–10}* On evening of Easter day: Luke 24.13–49
2 Easter	Acts 2.42–47 *Acts 2.14a, 22–32 {see below}*	1 Pet. 1.3–9	John 20.19–31
3 Easter	Acts 2.14, 22–33 *Acts 2.14, 36–41*	1 Pet. 1.17–21 *1 Pet. 1.17–23*	Luke 24.13–35
4 Easter	Acts 2.14, 36–41 *Acts 2.42–47*	1 Pet. 2.20–25 *1 Pet. 2.19–25*	John 10.1–10
5 Easter	Acts 6.1–7 *Acts 7.55–60*	1 Pet. 2.4–9 *1 Pet. 2.2–10*	John 14.1–12 *John 14.1–14*
6 Easter	Acts 8.5–8, 14–17 *Acts 17.22–31*	1 Pet. 3.15–18 *1 Pet. 3.13–22*	John 14.15–21
Ascension	Acts 1.1–11 *{Dan. 7.9–14}*	Eph. 1.17–23 *Eph. 1.15–23 {Acts 1.1–11}*	Matt. 28.16–20 *Luke 24.44–53*
7 Easter	Acts 1.12–14 *Acts 1.6–14*	1 Pet. 4.13–16 *1 Pet. 4.12–14; 5.6–11*	John 17.1–11
Pentecost Vigil	Gen. 11.1–9 or Exod. 19.3–8, 16–20 or Ezek. 37.1–14 or Joel 3.1–5	Rom. 8.22–27	John 7.37–39
Pentecost Day	Acts 2.1–11 *{Num. 11.24–30}*	1 Cor. 12.3–7 *1 Cor. 12.3b–13 {Acts 2.1–21}*	John 20.19–23 *{John 7.37–39}*

Table A2.1 (continued)

Sunday – Feast	First reading	Second reading	Gospel
Although not part of Eastertide, these feasts' occurrence is regulated by the date of Easter.			
Trinity Sunday	Exod. 34.4–6, 8–9	2 Cor. 13.11–13	John 3.16–18
	Gen. 1.1—2.4a		Matt. 28.16–20
	Isa. 40.12–17, 27–31		*CWL offers both ad lib.*
'Corpus Christi'[1]	Deut. 8.2–3, 14–16	1 Cor. 10.16–17	John 6.51–58
	Gen. 14.18–20	*1 Cor. 11.23–26*	
Sacred Heart of Jesus[2]	Deut. 7.6–11	1 John 4.7–16	Matt. 11.25–30

Readings for the Easter Vigil

For the Service of Readings at the Easter Vigil *RL* sets out a pattern of seven readings plus psalms or canticles, while *RCL* and *CWL* set out a pattern of nine; however, all three Lectionaries assume that in many instances this will be reduced, so all have set a minimum of three readings while requiring that Exodus 14—15 never be omitted.

Table A2.2 Readings for the Easter Vigil

Reading		Main text	Psalm / Canticle
RL	RCL/CWL		
1	1	Gen. 1.1—2.2	Ps. 104 [Ps. 33]
		Gen. 1.1—2.4a	*Ps. 136*
	2	Gen. 7.1–5, 11–18; 8.6–18; 9.8–13	Ps. 46
2	3	Gen. 22.1–18	Ps. 16
3	4	Exod. 14.15—15.1	Exod. 15.1–6, 17–18
		Exod. 14.10–31; 15.20–21	*Exod. 15.1b–13, 17–18*
4		Isa. 54.5–14	Ps. 30
5	5	Isa. 55.1–11	Isa. 12.2–6
6	6	Baruch 3.9–15, 32—4.4	Ps. 19
		{Prov. 8.1–8, 19–21; 9.4b–6}	
7	7	Ezek. 36.16–28	Ps. 42
		Ezek. 36.24–28	*Ps. 42 and 43*
	8	Ezek. 37.1–14	Ps. 143
	9	Zeph. 3.14–20	Ps. 98

[1] *RL* calls this festival 'The Body and Blood of Christ' with the status of 'solemnity'; *CWL* 'Day of Thanksgiving for the Institution of Holy Communion' with the status of 'optional festival'. It falls on the Thursday after Trinity Sunday but is, among Catholics, often transferred to the following Sunday thus destroying the logic of the Lectionary for Ordinary Time.

[2] This falls on the Friday after the Second Sunday after Pentecost, and does not usually interrupt the Lectionary sequence in Ordinary Time.

Old Testament readings for Sundays in Eastertide – *CWL* only

The *CWL* envisages a situation where some may 'require' an Old Testament reading and sets out the following with the proviso that 'if used, the reading from Acts must be used as the second reading'.

Table A2.3 Year A: *CWL* **Old Testament readings for Sundays in Eastertide**

Sunday	Reading
2 Easter	Exod. 14.10–31; 15.20–21
3 Easter	Zeph. 3.14–20
4 Easter	Gen. 7
5 Easter	Gen. 8.1–19
6 Easter	Gen. 8.20—9.17
7 Easter	Ezek. 36.24–28

Year B: 'The year of Mark'

Table A2.4 Year B: Readings for Lent and Eastertide

Sunday – Feast	First reading	Second reading	Gospel
Ash Wednesday	As Year A		
1 Lent	Gen. 9.8–15	1 Pet. 3.18–22	Mark 1.12–15
	Gen. 9.8–17		*Mark 1.9–15*
	Gen. 9.9–17		
2 Lent	Gen. 22.1–2,	Rom. 8.31–34	Mark 9.2–10
	9–13, 15–18	*Rom. 4.13–25*	*Mark 8.31–38*
	Gen. 17.1–7,		
	15–16		
3 Lent	Exod. 20.1–17	1 Cor. 1.22–25	John 2.13–25
		1 Cor. 1.18–25	*John 2.13–22*
4 Lent	2 Chron.	Eph. 2.4–10	John 3.14–21
	36.14–16, 19–23	*Eph. 2.1–10*	
	Num. 21.4–9		
Mothering Sunday	As Year A		
5 Lent	Jer. 31.31–34	Heb. 5.7–9	John 12.20–30
		Heb. 5.5–10	*John 12.20–33*
Palm Sunday	–	–	Mark 11.1–10 or
	As Year A	As Year A	John 12.12–16*
			Mark 14.1—15.47
Monday	As Year A		
Tuesday	As Year A		

---

* Gospel for use before the Procession with the Palms/**Liturgy of the Palms**: all three Lectionaries are identical.

Table A2.4 (continued)

Sunday – Feast	First reading	Second reading	Gospel
Wednesday	As Year A		
Maundy Thursday	As Year A		
Good Friday	As Year A		
Easter Eve	As Year A		
Easter Vigil	As Year A	As Year A	Mark 16.1–7/*1–8*
Easter Day	As Year A	As Year A	As Year A
	{Isa. 25.6–9}	*1 Cor. 15.1–11*	*{Mark 16.1–8}*
		{Acts 10.34–43}	
2 Easter	Acts 4.32–35	1 John 5.1–6	As Year A
	{see Table A2.5}	*1 John 1.1—2.2*	
3 Easter	Acts 3.13–15,	1 John 2.1–5	Luke 24.35–48
	17–19	*1 John 3.1–7*	*Luke 24.36b–48*
	Acts 3.12–19		
4 Easter	Acts 4.8–12	1 John 3.1–2	John 10.11–18
	Acts 4.5–12	1 John 3.18–24	
		1 John 3.16–24	
5 Easter	Acts 9.26–31	1 John 3.18–24	John 15.1–8
	Acts 8.26–40	*1 John 4.7–21*	
6 Easter	Acts 10.25–26,	1 John 4.7–10	John 15.9–17
	34–35, 44–48	*1 John 5.1–6*	
	Acts 10.44–48		
Ascension	As Year A	As Year A	Mark 16.15–20
		{RL only.	*As Year A*
		Eph. 4.1–13}	
7 Easter	Acts 1.15–17,	1 John 4.11–16	John 17.11–19
	20–26	*1 John 5.9–13*	*John 17.6–19*
	Acts 1.21–26		
Pentecost Vigil	As Year A		
Pentecost Day	As Year A	As year A	As Year A
	{Ezek. 37.1–14}	*{Gal. 5.16–25}*	*{John 15.26–27;*
		Rom. 8.22–27	*16.12–15}*
		{Acts 2.1–21}	*John 15.26–27;*
			16.4b–15
And:			
Trinity Sunday	Deut. 4.32–34,	Rom. 8.14–17	Matt. 28.16–20
	39–40	*Rom. 8.12–17*	*John 3.1–17*
	Isa. 6.1–8		
'Corpus Christi'	Exod. 24.3–8 /	Heb. 9.11–15 /	Mark 14.12–16,
	As Year A	*As Year A*	22–26 / *As Year A*
Sacred Heart	Hos. 11.1,	Eph. 3.8–12,	John 19.31–37
of Jesus[3]	3–4, 8–9	14–19	

---

[3] This falls on the Friday after the Second Sunday after Pentecost, and does not usually interrupt the Lectionary sequence in Ordinary Time.

Old Testament readings for Sundays in Eastertide – *CWL* only

Table A2.5 Year B: *CWL* Old Testament readings for Sundays in Eastertide

Sunday	Reading
2 Easter	As Year A
3 Easter	As Year A
4 Easter	Gen. 7.1–5, 11–18; 8.6–18; 9.8–13
5 Easter	Baruch 3.9–15, 32—4.4 or Gen. 22.1–18
6 Easter	Isa. 55.1–11
7 Easter	As Year A

Year C: 'The year of Luke'

Table A2.6 Year C: Readings for Lent and Eastertide

Sunday – feast	First reading	Second reading	Gospel
Ash Wednesday	As Year A		
1 Lent	Deut. 26.4–10	Rom. 10.8–13	Luke 4.1–13
	Deut. 26.1–11		
2 Lent	Gen. 15.5–12, 17–18	Phil. 3.17—4.1	Luke 9.28–36
	Gen. 15.1–12, 17–18		*Luke 13.31–35*
3 Lent	Exod. 3.1–8, 13–15	1 Cor. 10.1–6, 10–12	Luke 13.1–9
	Isa. 55.1–9	*1 Cor. 10.1–13*	
4 Lent	Josh. 5.9–12	2 Cor. 5.17–21	Luke 15.1–3, 11–32
		2 Cor. 5.16–21	
Mothering Sunday	*As Year A*		
5 Lent	Isa. 43.16–21	Phil. 3.8–14	John 8.1–11
		Phil. 3.4b–14	*John 12.1–8*
Palm Sunday	–	–	Luke 19.28–40*
	As Year A	As Year A	Luke 22.14—23.56
Monday	As Year A		
Tuesday	As Year A		
Wednesday	As Year A		
Maundy Thursday	As Year A		
Good Friday	As Year A		
Easter Eve	*As Year A*		
Easter Vigil	As Year A	As Year A	Luke 24.1–12

---

* Gospel for use before the Procession with the Palms/**Liturgy of the Palms**: all three Lectionaries are identical.

Table A2.6 (continued)

Sunday – feast	First reading	Second reading	Gospel
Easter Day	As Year A *{Isa. 65.17–25}*	As Year A *1 Cor. 15.19–26* *{Acts 10.34–43}*	As Year A *John 20.1–18* *{Luke 24.1–12}*
2 Easter	Acts 5.12–16 *Acts 5.27–32* *{see Table A2.7}*	Rev. 1.9–13. 17–19 *Rev. 1.4–8*	As Year A
3 Easter	Acts 5.27–32, 40–41 *Acts 9.1–6,* *[7–20]*	Rev. 5.11–14	John 21.1–19
4 Easter	Acts 13.14, 43–52 *Acts 9.36–43*	Rev. 7.9, 14–17 *Rev. 7.9–17*	John 10.27–30 *John 10.22–30*
5 Easter	Acts 14.21–27 *Acts 11.1–18*	Rev. 21.1–5 *Rev. 21.1–6*	John 13.31–35
6 Easter	Acts 15.1–2, 22–29 *Acts 16.9–15*	Rev. 21.10–14, 22–23 *Rev. 21.10,* *22—22.5*	John 14.23–29 *{John 5.1–9}*
Ascension	As Year A	As Year A {*RL* only: Heb. 9.24–28; 10.19–23}	Luke 24.46–53 *Luke 24.44–53*
7 Easter	Acts 7.55–60 *Acts 16.16–34*	Rev. 22.12–14, 16–17, 20 *Rev. 22.12–14,* *16–17, 20–21*	John 17.20–26
Pentecost Vigil	As Year A		
Pentecost Day	As Year A *{Gen. 11.1–9}*	As Year A {Rom. 8.8–17} *Rom. 8.14–17* *{Acts 2.1–21}*	As Year A {John 14.15–16, 23–26} *John 14.8–17,* *[25–27]*
And:			
Trinity Sunday	Prov. 8.22–31 *Prov. 8.1–4,* *22–31*	Rom. 5.1–5	John 16.12–15
'Corpus Christi'	Gen. 14.18–20 = *CWL*	1 Cor. 11.23–26 = *CWL*	Luke 9.11–17 *As Year A*
Sacred Heart of Jesus[4]	Ezek. 34.11–16	Rom. 5.5–11	Luke 15.3–7

---

[4] This falls on the Friday after the Second Sunday after Pentecost, and does not usually interrupt the Lectionary sequence in Ordinary Time.

Old Testament readings for Sundays in Eastertide – *CWL* only

Table A2.7 Year C: *CWL* Old Testament readings for Sundays in Eastertide

Sunday	Reading
2 Easter	As Year A
3 Easter	As Year A
4 Easter	As Year B
5 Easter	As Year B
6 Easter	Ezek. 37.1–14
7 Easter	As Year A

Appendix 3

The sequence of Gospels, with related first readings, in Ordinary Time

See Appendix 1 for a guide to codes used here.

Year A: 'The year of Matthew'

Table A3.1 Year A: Gospels and first readings in Ordinary Time

Sunday	Gospel	First reading
	Lectionary unit 1	
1 / 1 AE*	Matt. 3.13–17	Isa. 42.1–4, 6–7
		Isa. 42.1–9
2 / 2 AE	John 1.29–34	Isa. 49.3, 5–6
	John 1.29–42	*Isa. 49.1–7*
	Lectionary unit 2	
3 / 3 AE	Matt. 4.12–23	Isa. 8.23—9.3
		Isa. 9.1–4
4 / 4 AE	Matt. 5.1–12	Zeph. 2.3; 3.12–13
	John 2.1–11	Mic. 6.1–8
		1 Kings 17.8–16
5 / P1	Matt. 5.13–16	Isa. 58.7–10
	Matt. 5.13–20	Isa. 58.1–9a, [9b–12]
		Isa. 58.1–12
6 / P2	Matt. 5.17–37	Ecclus. 15.15–20
	Matt. 5.21–37	Deut. 30.15–20
		Both offered as options
7 / P3	Matt. 5.38–48	Lev. 19.1–2, 17–18
		Lev. 19.1–2, 9–18
8	Matt. 6.24–34	Isa. 49.14–15
		Isa. 49.8–16a
/ 2BL	*Matt. 6.24–34*	*Gen. 1.1—2.3*
/ 1BL	*Matt. 17.1–9*	*Exod. 24.12–18*
9 / P4	Matt. 7.21–27	Deut. 11.18, 26–28, 32
	Matt. 7.21–29	*RCL moves to different strategy until Sunday 33 – see Appendix 5*
		Deut. 18–21, 26–28

---

* *RCL* and *CWL* use a different numbering system for the Sundays between Christmastide and Lent, but have the same readings on the same days.

Table A3.1 (continued)

Sunday	Gospel	First reading
	Lectionary unit 3	
10 / P5	Matt. 9.9–13	Hos. 6.3–6
	Matt. 9.9–13, 18–26	*Hos. 5.15—6.6*
11 / P6	Matt. 9.36—10.8	Exod. 19.2–6
	Matt. 9.35—10.8 [9–23]	*Exod. 19.2–8a*
12 / P7	Matt. 10.26–33	Jer. 20.10–13
	Matt. 10.24–39	*Jer. 20.7–13*
13 / P8	Matt. 10.37–42	2 Kings 4.8–11, 14–16
	Matt. 10.40–42	*Jer. 28.5–9*
	Lectionary unit 4	
14 / P9	Matt. 11.25–30	Zech. 9.9–10
	Matt. 11.16–19, 25–30	*Zech. 9.9–12*
15 / P10	Matt. 13.1–23	Isa. 55.10–11
	Matt. 13.1–9, 18–23	*Isa. 55.10–13*
16 / P11	Matt. 13.24–43	Wisd. 12.13, 16–19
	Matt. 13.24–30, 36–43	
17 / P12	Matt. 13.44–52	1 Kings 3.5, 7–12
	Matt. 13.31–33, 44–52	
	Lectionary unit 5	
18 / P13	Matt. 14.13–21	Isa. 55.1–3
		Isa. 55.1–5
19 / P14	Matt. 14.22–33	1 Kings 19.9,
		11–13 / *9–18*
20 / P15	Matt. 15.21–28	Isa. 56.1, 6–7
	Matt. 15.[10–20,] 21–28	*Isa. 56.6–8*
21 / P16	Matt. 16.13–20	Isa. 22.19–23
		Isa. 51.1–6
22 / P17	Matt. 16.21–27	Jer. 20.7–9
	Matt. 16.21–28	*Jer. 15.15–21*
23 / P18	Matt. 18.15–20	Ezek. 33.7–9
		Ezek. 33.7–11
24 / P19	Matt. 18.21–35	Ecclus. 27.30—28.7
		Gen. 50.15–21
	Lectionary unit 6	
25 / P20	Matt. 20.1–16	Isa. 55.6–9
		Jonah 3.10—4.11
26 / P21	Matt. 21.28–32	Ezek. 18.25–28
	Matt. 21.23–32	*Ezek. 18.1–4, 25–32*
27 / P22	Matt. 21.33–43	Isa. 5.1–7
	Matt. 21.33–46	
28 / P23	Matt. 22.1–14	Isa. 25.6–10
		Isa. 25.1–9
29 / P24	Matt. 22.15–21	Isa. 45.1, 4–6
	Matt. 22.15–22	*Isa. 45.1–7*

Table A3.1 (continued)

Sunday	Gospel	First reading
30 / P25	Matt. 22.34–40	Exod. 22.20–26
	Matt. 22.34–46	*Lev. 19.1–2, 15–18*
31 / 4BA	Matt. 23.1–12	Mal. 1.14—2.2, 8–10
	Matt. 24.1–14	*Mic. 3.5–12*
32 / 3BA	Matt. 25.1–13	Wisd. 6.12–16
		{*Amos 5.18–24*}
33 / 2BA	Matt. 25.14–30	Prov. 31.10–31 (bits)
		Zeph. 1.7, 12–18
	Lectionary unit 7	
34 – Christ the	Matt. 25.31–46	Ezek. 34.11–12, 15–17
King / 1BA		*Ezek. 34.11–16, 20–24*
Harvest Thanksgiving	*Luke 12.16–30 or 17.11–19*	*Deut. 8.7–18 or 28.1–14*
Bible Sunday	*Matt. 24.30–35*	*Neh. 8.1–4a, [5–6,] 8–12*
Dedication Festival	*Matt. 21.12–16*	*1 Kings 8.22–30 or*
		Rev. 21.9–14

Year B: 'The year of Mark'

Table A3.2 Year B: Gospels and first readings in Ordinary Time

Sunday	Gospel	First reading
	Lectionary unit 1	
1 / 1 AE	Mark 1.6b–11	Isa. 55.1–11
	Mark 1.4–11	*Gen. 1.1–5*
2 / 2 AE	John 1.35–42	1 Sam. 3.3–10, 19
	John 1.43–51	*1 Sam. 3.1–10, [11–20]*
	Lectionary unit 2 – stage 1	
3 / 3 AE	Mark 1.14–20	Jonah 3.1–5, 10
	John 2.1–11	*Gen. 14.17–20*
4 / 4 AE	Mark 1.21–28	Deut. 18.15–20
5 / P1	Mark 1.29–39	Job 7.1–4, 6–7
		Isa. 40.21–31
6 / P2	Mark 1.40–45	Lev. 13.1–2, 45–46
		2 Kings 5.1–14
7 / P3	Mark 2.1–12	Isa. 43.18–19, 21–22, 24–25
		Isa. 43.18–25
8 /	Mark 2.18–22	Hos. 2.16–17, 21–22
	Mark 2.13–22	Hos. 2.14–20
/ 2BL	*John 1.1–14*	*Prov. 8.1, 22–32*
/ 1BL	**Mark 1.9–15**	**Gen. 9.8–17**
	Mark 9.2–9	*2 Kings 2.1–12*

Table A3.2 (continued)

Sunday	Gospel	First reading
9 / P4	Mark 2.23—3.6	Deut. 5.12–15
		RCL moves to different strategy until Sunday 33 – see Appendix 5
	Lectionary unit 2 – stage 2	
10 / P5	Mark 3.20–35	Gen. 3.9–15
		Gen. 3.8–15
11 / P6	Mark 4.26–34	Ezek. 17.22–24
12 / P7	Mark 4.35–41	Job 38.1, 8–11
13 / P8	Mark 5.21–43	Wisd. 1.13–15; 2.23–24
		{Lam. 3.22–33}
14 / P9	Mark 6.1–6	Ezek. 2.2–5 / *1–5*
	Mark 6.1–13	
	Lectionary unit 2 – stage 3	
15 / P10	Mark 6.7–13	Amos 7.12–15
	Mark 6.14–29	*Amos 7.7–15*
16 / P11	Mark 6.30–34, 53–56	Jer. 23.1–6
17 / P12	John 6.1–15	2 Kings 4.42–44
	John 6.1–21	
18 / P13	John 6.24–35	Exod. 16.2–4, 12–15
		Exod. 16.2–4, 9–15
19 / P14	John 6.41–52	1 Kings 19.4–8
	John 6.35, 41–51	
20 / P15	John 6.51–58	Prov. 9.1–6
21 / P16	John 6.61–70	Josh. 24.1–2, 15–18
	John 6.56–69	*Josh. 24.1–2, 14–18*
22 / P17	Mark 7.1–8, 14–15, 21	Deut. 4.1–2, 6–8
	Mark 7.1–8, 14–15, 21–23	*Deut. 4.1–2, 6–9*
23 / P18	Mark 7.31–37	Isa. 35.4–7
	Mark 7.24–37	
	Lectionary unit 3 – stage 1	
24 / P19	Mark 8.27–35	Isa. 50.5–9
	Mark 8.27–38	*Isa. 50.4–9a*
25 / P20	Mark 9.30–37	Wisd. 2.12, 17–20
		Wisd. 1.16—2.1, 12–22
		{Jer. 11.18–20}
26 / P21	Mark 9.37–42, 44, 46–47	Num. 11.25–29
	Mark 9.38–50	*Num. 11.4–6, 10–16, 24–29*
27 / P22	Mark 10.2–16	Gen. 2.18–24
28 / P23	Mark 10.17–30	Wisd. 7.7–11
	Mark 10.17–31	*Amos 5.6–7, 10–15*
29 / P24	Mark 10.35–45	Isa. 53.10–11
		Isa. 53.4–12
30 / P25	Mark 10.46–52	Jer. 31.7–9

Table A3.2 (continued)

Sunday	Gospel	First reading
	Lectionary unit 3 – stage 2	
31 / 4BA	Mark 12.28–34	Deut. 6.2–6
		Deut. 6.1–9
32 / 3BA	Mark 12.38–44	1 Kings 17.10–16
	Mark 1.14–20	*Jonah 3.1–5, 10*
33 / 2BA	Mark 13.24–32	Dan. 12.1–3
	Mark 13.1–8	
	Lectionary unit 3 – stage 3	
34 – Christ the	John 18.33–37	Dan. 7.13–14
King / 1 BA		*Dan. 7.9–10, 13–14*
Harvest Thanksgiving	*Matt. 6.25–33*	*Joel 2.21–27*
Bible Sunday	*John 5.36b–47*	*Isa. 55.1–11*
Dedication Festival	*John 10.22–29*	*Gen. 28.11–18 or*
		Rev. 21.9–14

Year C: 'The year of Luke'

Table A3.3 Year C: Gospels and first readings in Ordinary Time

Sunday	Gospel	First reading
	Lectionary unit 1	
1 / 1AE	Luke 3.15–16, 21–22	Isa. 40.1–5, 9–11
	Luke 3.15–17, 21–22	*Isa. 43.1–7*
2 / 2AE	John 2.1–12	Isa. 62.1–5
	John 2.1–11	
	Lectionary unit 2	
3 / 3AE	Luke 1.1–4; 4.14–21	Neh. 8.2–6, 8–10
	Luke 4.14–21	*Neh. 8.1–3, 5–6, 8–10*
4 / 4AE	Luke 4.21–30	Jer. 1.4–5, 17–19
	Luke 4.22–40	*Jer. 1.4–10*
		Ezek. 43.27—44.4
	Lectionary unit 3	
5 / P1	Luke 5.1–11	Isa. 6.1–8
		Isa. 6.1–8, [9–13]
6 / P2	Luke 6.17, 20–26	Jer. 17.5–8
	Luke 6.17–26	*Jer. 17.5–10*
7 / P3	Luke 6.27–38	1 Sam. 26.2, 7–9,
		12–13, 22–23
		Gen. 45.3–11, 15
8	Luke 6.39–45	Ecclus. 27.4–7
	Luke 6.39–49	*Isa. 55.10–13*

Table A3.3 (continued)

Sunday	Gospel	First reading
/ 2BL	*Luke 8.22–25*	*Gen. 2.4b–9, 15–25*
/ 1BL	**Luke 9.28–36, [37–43]**	**Exod. 34.29–35**
9 / P4	Luke 7.1–10	1 Kings 8.41–43
		RCL moves to different strategy until Sunday 33 – see Appendix 5
		1 Kings 8.22–23, 41–43
10 / P5	Luke 7.11–17	1 Kings 17.17–24
11 / P6	Luke 7.36—8.3	2 Sam. 12.7–10, 13
		2 Sam. 11.26—12.10, 13–15
12 / P7	Luke 9.18–24	Zech. 12.10–11
	Luke 8.26–39	*Isa. 65.1–9*
	Lectionary unit 4	
13 / P8	Luke 9.51–62	1 Kings 19.16, 19–21
		1 Kings 19.15–16, 19–21
14 / P9	Luke 10.1–12, 17–20	Isa. 66.10–14
	Luke 10.1–10, 16–20	
15 / P10	Luke 10.25–37	Deut. 30.10–14
		Deut. 30.9–14
16 / P11	Luke 10.38–42	Gen. 18.1–10
17 / P12	Luke 11.1–13	Gen. 18.20–32
18 / P13	Luke 12.13–21	Eccles. 1.2; 2.21–23
		Eccles. 1.2, 12–14; 2.18–23
19 / P14	Luke 12.32–48	Wisd. 18.6–9
	Luke 12.32–40	*Gen. 15.1–6*
20 / P15	Luke 12.49–53	Jer. 38.4–6, 8–10
	Luke 12.49–56	*Jer. 23.23–29*
21 / P16	Luke 13.22–30	Isa. 66.18–21
	Luke 13.10–17	*Isa. 58.9b–14*
22 / P17	Luke 14.1, 7–14	Ecclus. 3.17–20, 28–29
		Ecclus. 10.12–18
		{Prov. 25.6–7}
23 / P18	Luke 14.25–33	Wisd. 9.13–18
		Deut. 30.15–20
	Lectionary unit 5	
24 / P19	Luke 15.1–32	Exod. 32.7–11, 13–14
	Luke 15.1–10	*Exod. 32.7–14*
	Lectionary unit 6	
25 / P20	Luke 16.1–13	Amos 8.4–7
26 / P21	Luke 16.19–31	Amos 6.1, 4–7
27 / P22	Luke 17.5–10	Hab. 1.2–3; 2.2–4
		Hab. 1.1–4; 2.1–4
28 / P23	Luke 17.11–19	2 Kings 5.14–17
		2 Kings 5.1–3, 7–15c

Table A3.3 (continued)

Sunday	Gospel	First reading
29 / P24	Luke 18.1–8	Exod. 17.8–13
		Gen. 32.22–31
30 / P25	Luke 18.9–14	Ecclus. 35.12–14, 16–19
		{Jer. 14.7–10, 19–22}
31 / 4BA	Luke 19.1–10	Wisd. 11.22—12.2
		Isa. 1.10–18
	Lectionary unit 7	
32 / 3BA	Luke 20.27–38	2 Macc. 7.1–2, 9–14
		Job 19.23–27a
33 / 2BA	Luke 21.5–19	Mal. 3.19–20
		Mal. 4.1–2a
	Lectionary unit 8	
34 Christ the King / 1BA	Luke 23.35–43	2 Sam. 5.1–3
		Jer. 23.1–6
Harvest Thanksgiving	*John 6.25–35*	*Deut. 26.1–11*
Bible Sunday	*Luke 4.16–24*	*Isa. 45.22–25*
Dedication Festival	*John 2.13–22*	*1 Chron. 29.6–9*

Appendix 4

The sequence of second readings in Ordinary Time

The purpose of these tables is to show at a glance the sweep of 'semi-continuous reading' of New Testament readings, outside of the Gospels, in Ordinary Time. We must remember, of course, that this sweep is always interrupted by Lent and Eastertide. In *CWL* this is also interrupted by the retention of a pre-Lent period (2BL and 1BL below) now known as 'Second Sunday before Lent' and the 'Sunday next before Lent'; and in *RCL* by its having 1BL (> Buxton 2002).

See Appendix 1 for a guide to codes used here.

Year A

Table A4.1 Year A: Second readings in Ordinary Time

Sunday	Reading
1[1]	Acts 10.34–38
	Acts 10.34–43
2	1 Cor. 1.1–3
	1 Cor. 1.1–9
3	1 Cor. 1.10–13, 17
	1 Cor. 1.10–18
4	1 Cor. 1.26–31
	1 Cor. 1.18–31
5	1 Cor. 2.1–5
	1 Cor. 2.1–12 [13–16]
6	1 Cor. 2.6–10
	1 Cor. 3.1–9
7	1 Cor. 3.16–23
	1 Cor. 3.10–11, 16–23
8	1 Cor. 4.1–5
/ 2BL	*Rom. 8.18–25*
/ 1BL	*2 Pet. 1.16–21*

---

[1] The *CWL* system for referring to the Sundays (e.g. 'after Epiphany', 'before Lent' etc.) is not used here as it is irrelevant to this sequence of semi-continuous reading. When a particular Sunday falls within the *CWL* system can be found by looking at the number of that Sunday in Appendix 3.

Table A4.1 (continued)

Sunday	Reading
9	Rom. 3.21–25, 28
	Rom. 1.16–17; 3.22b–28 [29–31]
10	Rom. 4.18–25
	Rom. 4.13–25
11	Rom. 5.6–11
	Rom. 5.1–8
12	Rom. 5.12–15
	Rom. 6.1b–11
13	Rom. 6.3–4, 8–11
	Rom. 6.12–23
14	Rom. 8.9, 11–13
	Rom. 7.15–25a
15	Rom. 8.18–23
	Rom. 8.1–11
16	Rom. 8.26–27
	Rom. 8.12–25
17	Rom. 8.28–30
	Rom. 8.26–39
18	Rom. 8.35, 37–39
	Rom. 9.1–5
19	Rom. 9.1–5
	Rom. 10.5–15
20	Rom. 11.13–15, 29–32
	Rom. 11.13–16, 29–32
	Rom. 11.1–2a, 29–32
21	Rom. 11.33–36
	Rom. 12.1–8
22	Rom. 12.1–2
	Rom. 12.9–21
23	Rom. 13.8–10
	Rom. 13.8–14
24	Rom. 14.7–9
	Rom. 14.1–12
25	Phil. 1.20–24, 27
	Phil. 1.21–30
26	Phil. 2.1–11
	Phil. 2.1–13
27	Phil. 4.6–9
	Phil. 3.4b–14
28	Phil. 4.12–14, 19–20
	Phil. 4.1–9
29	1 Thess. 1.1–5
	1 Thess. 1.1–10
30	1 Thess. 1.5–10
	1 Thess. 2.1–8

Table A4.1 (continued)

Sunday	Reading
31	1 Thess. 2.7–9, 13
	1 Thess. 2.9–13
32	1 Thess. 4.13–18
33	1 Thess. 5.1–6
	1 Thess. 5.1–11
34 Christ the King	1 Cor. 15.20–26, 28
	Eph. 1.15–23
Harvest Thanksgiving	*2 Cor. 9.6–15*
Bible Sunday	*Col. 3.12–17*
Dedication Festival	*Heb. 12.18–24*

Year B

Table A4.2 Year B: Second readings in Ordinary Time

Sunday	Reading
1	1 John 5.1–9
	Acts 19.1–7
2	1 Cor. 6.13–15, 17–20
	1 Cor. 6.12–20
	Rev. 5.1–10
3	1 Cor. 7.29–31
	Rev. 19.6–10
4	1 Cor. 7.32–35
	1 Cor. 8.1–13
	Rev. 12.1–5a
5	1 Cor. 9.16–19, 22–23
	1 Cor. 9.16–23
6	1 Cor. 10.31—11.1
	1 Cor. 9.24–27
7	2 Cor. 1.18–22
8	2 Cor. 3.1–6
/ 2BL	*Col. 1.15–20*
/ 1BL	*1 Pet. 3.18–22*
	2 Cor. 4.3–6
9	2 Cor. 4.6–11
	2 Cor. 4.5–12
10	2 Cor. 4.13—5.1
11	2 Cor. 5.6–10
	2 Cor. 5.[11–13,] 14–17
12	2 Cor. 5.14–17
	2 Cor. 6.1–13
13	2 Cor. 8.7, 9, 13–15
	2 Cor. 8.7–15

Table A4.2 (continued)

Sunday	Reading
14	2 Cor. 12.7–10
	2 Cor. 12.2–10
15	Eph. 1.3–14
16	Eph. 2.13–18
	Eph. 2.11–22
17	Eph. 4.1–6
	Eph. 3.14–21
18	Eph. 4.17, 20–24
	Eph. 4.1–16
19	Eph. 4.30—5.2
	Eph. 4.25—5.2
20	Eph. 5.15–20
21	Eph. 5.21–32
	Eph. 6.10–20
22	Jas. 1.17–18, 21–22, 27
	Jas. 1.17–27
23	Jas. 2.1–5
	Jas. 2.1–10, [11–13,] 14–17
24	Jas. 2.14–18
	Jas. 3.1–12
25	Jas. 3.16—4.3
	Jas. 3.13—4.3, 7–8a
26	Jas. 5.1–6
	Jas. 5.13–20
27	Heb. 2.9–11
	Heb. 1.1–4; 2.5–12
28	Heb. 4.12–13
	Heb. 4.12–16
29	Heb. 4.14–16
	Heb. 5.1–10
30	Heb. 5.1–6
	Heb. 7.23–28
31	Heb. 7.23–28
	Heb. 9.11–14
32	Heb. 9.24–28
33	Heb. 10.11–14, 18
	Heb. 10.11–18
	Heb. 10.11–14, [15–18,] 19–25
34 Christ the King	Rev. 1.5–8
	Rev. 1.4b–8
Harvest Thanksgiving	*1 Tim. 2.1–7 or 6.6–10*
Bible Sunday	*2 Tim. 3.14—4.5*
Dedication Festival	*1 Pet. 2.1–10*

Year C

Table A4.3 Year C: Second readings in Ordinary Time

Sunday	Reading
1	Titus 2.11–14; 3.4–7
	Acts 8.14–17
2	1 Cor. 12.4–11
	1 Cor. 12.1–11
3	1 Cor. 12.12–30
	1 Cor. 12.12–31a
4	1 Cor. 12.31—13.13
	1 Cor. 13.1–13
5	1 Cor. 15.1–11
6	1 Cor. 15.12, 16–20
	1 Cor. 15.12–20
7	1 Cor. 15.45–49
	1 Cor. 15.35–38, 42–50
8	1 Cor. 15.54–58
	1 Cor. 15.51–58
/ 2BL	Rev. 4
/ 1BL	*2 Cor. 3.12—4.2*
9	Gal. 1.1–2, 6–10
	Gal. 1.1–12
10	Gal. 1.11–19
	Gal. 1.11–24
11	Gal. 2.16, 19–21
	Gal. 2.15–21
12	Gal. 3.26–29
	Gal. 3.23–29
13	Gal. 5.1, 13–18
	Gal. 5.1, 13–25
14	Gal. 6.14–18
	Gal. 6.[1–6,] 7–16
15	Col. 1.15–20
	Col. 1.1–14
16	Col. 1.24–28
	Col. 1.15–28
17	Col. 2.12–14
	Col. 2.6–15, [16–19]
18	Col. 3.1–5, 9–11
	Col. 3.1–11
19	Heb. 11.1–2, 8–19
	Heb. 11.1–3, 8–16
20	Heb. 12.1–4
	Heb. 11.29—12.2

Table A4.3 (continued)

Sunday	Reading
21	Heb. 12.5–7, 11–13
	Heb. 12.18–29
22	Heb. 12.18–19, 22–24
	Heb. 13.1–8, 15–16
23	Philem. 9–10; 12–17
	Philem. 1–21
24	1 Tim. 1.12–17
25	1 Tim. 2.1–8
	1 Tim. 2.1–7
26	1 Tim. 6.11–16
	1 Tim. 6.6–19
27	2 Tim. 1.6–8, 13–14
	2 Tim. 1.1–14
28	2 Tim. 2.8–13
	2 Tim. 2.8–15
29	2 Tim. 3.14—4.2
	2 Tim. 3.14—4.5
30	2 Tim. 4.6–8, 16–18
31	2 Thess. 1.11—2.2
	2 Thess. 1.1–4, 11–12
	2 Thess. 1.1–12
32	2 Thess. 2.16—3.5
	2 Thess. 2.1–5, 13–17
33	2 Thess. 3.7–12
	2 Thess. 3.6–13
34 Christ the King	Col. 1.11–20
Harvest Thanksgiving	*Phil. 4.4–9 or Rev. 14.14–18*
Bible Sunday	*Rom. 15.1–6*
Dedication Festival	*Eph. 2.19–22*

Appendix 5

The sequence of semi-continuous first readings in Ordinary Time in *RCL* (and optionally in *CWL*)

Year A

Table A5.1 Year A: Semi-continuous first readings in Ordinary Time

Sunday	
P4	Gen. 6.9–22; 7.24; 8.14–19
P5	Gen. 12.1–9
P6	Gen. 18.1–15; [21.1–7]
P7	Gen. 21.8–21
P8	Gen. 22.1–14
P9	Gen. 24.34–38, 42–49, 58–67
P10	Gen. 25.19–34
P11	Gen. 28.1–19a
P12	Gen. 29.15–28
P13	Gen. 32.22–31
P14	Gen. 37.1–4, 12–28
P15	Gen. 45.1–15
P16	Exod. 1.8—2.10
P17	Exod. 3.1–15
P18	Exod. 12.1–14
P19	Exod. 14.19–31, [15.1b–11, 20–21]
P20	Exod. 16.2–15
P21	Exod. 17.1–7
P22	Exod. 20.1–4, 7–9, 12–20
P23	Exod. 32.1–14
P24	Exod. 33.12–23
P25	Deut. 34.1–12
P26	*RCL only*: Josh. 3.7–17
P27	*RCL only*: Josh. 24.1–3a, 14–25
P28	*RCL only*: Judg. 4.1–7

Year B

Table A5.2 Year B: Semi-continuous first readings in Ordinary Time

Sunday	
P4	1 Sam. 3.1–10, [11–20]
P5	1 Sam. 8.4–11, [12–15,] 16–20; [11.14–15]
P6	1 Sam. 15.34—16.13
P7	1 Sam. 17.[1a, 4–11, 19–23,] 32–49
	{1 Sam. 17.57—18.5, 10–16}
P8	2 Sam. 1.1, 17–27
P9	2 Sam. 5.1–5, 9–10
P10	2 Sam. 6.1–5, 12b–19
P11	2 Sam. 7.1–14a
P12	2 Sam. 11.1–15
P13	2 Sam. 11.26—12.13a
P14	2 Sam. 18.5–9, 15, 31–33
P15	1 Kings 2.10–12; 3.3–14
P16	1 Kings 8.[1, 6, 10–11,] 22–30, 41–43
P17	Song of Sol. 2.8–13
P18	Prov. 22.1–2, 8–9, 22–23
P19	Prov. 1.20–33
P20	Prov. 31.10–31
P21	Esth. 7.1–6, 9–10; 9.20–22
P22	Job 1.1; 2.1–10
P23	Job 23.1–9, 16–17
P24	Job 38.1–7, [34–41]
P25	Job 42.1–6, 10–17
P26	*RCL only*: Ruth 1.1–18
P27	*RCL only*: Ruth 3.1–5; 4.13–17
P28	*RCL only*: 1 Sam. 1.4–20

Year C

Table A5.3 Year C: Semi-continuous first readings in Ordinary Time

Sunday	
P4	1 Kings 18.20–21, [22–29,] 30–39
P5	1 Kings 17.8–16, [17–24]
P6	1 Kings 21.1–10, [11–14,] 15–21a
P7	1 Kings 19.1–4, [5–7,] 8–15a
P8	2 Kings 2.1–2, 6–14
P9	2 Kings 5.1–14
P10	Amos 7.7–17
P11	Amos 8.1–12
P12	Hosea 1.2–10
P13	Hosea 11.1–11
P14	Isa. 1.1, 10–20
P15	Isa. 5.1–7
P16	Jer. 1.4–10
P17	Jer. 2.4–13
P18	Jer. 18.1–11
P19	Jer. 4.11–12, 22–28
P20	Jer. 8.18—9.1
P21	Jer. 32.1–3a, 6–15
P22	Lam. 1.1–6
P23	Jer. 29.1, 4–7
P24	Jer. 31.27–34
P25	Joel 2.23–32
P26	*RCL only*: Hab. 1.1–4; 2.1–4
P27	*RCL only*: Hag. 1.15b—2.9
P28	*RCL only*: Isa. 65.17–25

Appendix 6

The Lectionaries replaced
by *RL* and *CWL*

This listing does not contain the readings for all the days listed in either of the sixteenth-century books, but rather concentrates on those days for which there is an equivalent in Appendices 1–3.

A glance down the table shows that the BCP uses virtually the same *set* of pericopes, but these have often been displaced so that they occur sometimes a week or a fortnight later than in the 1570 Roman Missal (commonly called 'the Tridentine Missal').

Note the virtual absence of readings from the Old Testament; and also of readings from the New Testament apart from the Gospels and the Pauline letters.

Table A6.1 Comparison of the Tridentine Missal (*MR*) and the BCP

	Tridentine Missal		BCP	
Day	Epistle	Gospel	Epistle	Gospel
1 Advent	Rom. 13.11–14a	Luke 21.25–33	Rom. 13.8–14	Matt. 21.1–13
2 Advent	Rom. 15.4–13	Matt. 11.2–10	ditto	Luke 21.25–33
3 Advent	Phil. 4.4–7	John 1.19–28	1 Cor. 4.1–5	Matt. 11.2–10
4 Advent	1 Cor. 4.1–5	Luke 3.1–6	Phil. 4.4–7	John 1.19–28
Christmas	Titus 2.11–15	Luke 2.1–14		
	Titus 3.4–7	Luke 2.15–20		
	Heb. 1.1–12	John 1.1–14	ditto	ditto
1 AC	Gal. 4.1–7	Luke 2.33–40	ditto	Matt. 1.18–25
Circumcision	Titus 2.11–15	Luke 2.21	Rom. 4.8–14	Luke 2.15–21
Epiphany	Isa. 60.1–6	Matt. 2.1–12	Eph. 3.1–12	ditto
1 AE	Rom. 12.1–5	Luke 2.42–52	ditto	Luke 2.41–52
2 AE	Rom. 12.6–16	John 2.1–11	ditto	ditto
3 AE	Rom. 12.16–21	Matt. 8.1–13	ditto	ditto
4 AE	Rom. 13.8–10	Matt. 8.23–27	Rom. 13.1–7	Matt. 8.23–34
5 AE	Col. 3.12–17	Matt. 13.24–30	ditto	ditto
6 AE	1 Thess. 1.2–10	Matt. 13.31–35	1 John 3.1–8	Matt. 24.23–31
7-gesima	1 Cor. 9.24–27; 10.1–5	Matt. 20.1–16	1 Cor. 9.24–27	ditto
6-gesima	2 Cor. 11.19–33; 12.1–9	Luke 8.4–15	2 Cor. 11.19–31	ditto
5-gesima	1 Cor. 13.1–13	Luke 18.31–43	ditto	ditto

Table A6.1 (continued)

Day	Tridentine Missal		BCP	
	Epistle	Gospel	Epistle	Gospel
Ashes	Joel 2.12–19	Matt. 6.16–21	Joel 2.12–17	ditto
1 Lent	2 Cor. 6.1–10	Matt. 4.1–11	ditto	ditto
2 Lent	1 Thess. 4.1–7	Matt. 17.1–9	1 Thess. 4.1–8	Matt. 15.21–28
3 Lent	Eph. 5.1–9	Luke 11.14–28	Eph. 5.1–14	ditto
4 Lent	Gal. 4.22–31	John 6.1–15	Gal. 4.21–31	John 6.1–14
5 Lent	Heb. 9.11–15	John 8.46–59	ditto	ditto
Palm	Phil. 2.5–11	Matt. 26.1–27.66	ditto	Matt. 27.1–55
Monday	Isa. 50.5–10	John 12.1–9	Isa. 63.1–19	Mark 14.1–72
Tuesday	Jer. 11.18–20	Mark 14.1–15.46	Isa. 50.5–11	Mark 15.1–39
Wednesday	Isa. 62.11; 63.1–7 & Isa. 53.1–12	Luke 22.1–23.53	Heb. 9.16–28	Luke 22.1–71
Thursday	1 Cor. 11.20–32	John 13.1–15	1 Cor. 11.17–34	Luke 23.1–49
G. Friday	Hos. 6.1–6 & Exod. 12.1–11	John 18.1–19.42	Heb. 10.1–25	John 19.1–37
Saturday*	Col. 3.1–4**	Matt. 23.1–7	1 Pet. 3.17–22	Matt. 27.57–66
Easter	1 Cor. 5.7–8	Mark 15.1–7	Col. 3.1–7	John 20.1–10

---

* Comparison is not really possible on this day. *MR* actually celebrated the Easter Vigil early on the Saturday morning (because of fasting regulations) and hence its texts are Easter texts; BCP celebrated this Saturday in real time, and hence its texts are still Lenten – and it did not envisage an Easter Vigil in either real or notional time.

** In addition there were the twelve 'prophecies': Gen. 1.1—2.2; Gen. 5—8; Gen. 22.1–19; Exod. 14.24—15.1; Isa. 54.17—55.11; Baruch 3.9–38; Ezek. 37.1–14; Isa. 4.1–6; Exod. 12.1–11; Jonah 3.1–10; Deut. 31.22–30; Dan. 3.1–24.

1 PE	1 John 5.4–10	John 20.19–31	1 John 5.4–12	John 20.19–23
2 PE	1 Pet. 2.21–25	John 10.10–16	ditto	ditto
3 PE	1 Pet. 2.11–19	John 16.16–22	1 Pet. 2.11–17	ditto
4 PE	Jas. 1.17–21	John 16.5–14	ditto	ditto
5 PE	Jas. 1.22–27	John 16.23–30	ditto	John 16.23–33
Ascension	Acts 1.1–11	Mark 16.14–20	ditto	ditto
6 PE	1 Pet. 4.7–11	John 15.26–6.4	ditto	ditto
Pentecost	Acts 2.1–11	John 14.23–31	ditto	John 14.15–31
Trinity	Rom. 11.33–36	Matt. 28.18–20	Rev. 4.1–11	John 3.1–15
1 AP***	1 John 4.8–21	Luke 6.36–42		
Corpus Christi	1 Cor. 11.23–29	John 6.56–59		
2 AP 1 AT	1 John 3.13–18	Luke 14.16–24	1 John 4.7–21	Luke 16.19–31
3 AP 2 AT	1 Pet. 5.6–11	Luke 15.1–10	1 John 3.13–24	Luke 14.16–24
4 AP 3 AT	Rom. 8.18–23	Luke 5.1–11	1 Pet. 5.1–11	ditto
5 AP 4 AT	1 Pet. 3.8–15	Matt. 5.20–24	ditto	Luke 6.36–42
6 AP 5 AT	Rom. 6.3–11	Mark 8.1–9	ditto	Luke 5.1–11
7 AP 6 AT	Rom. 6.19–23	Matt. 7.15–21	Rom. 6.3–11	Matt. 5.20–26
8 AP 7 AT	Rom. 8.12–17a	Luke 16.1–9	Rom. 6.19–23	Mark 8.1–9
9 AP 8 AT	1 Cor. 10.6–13	Luke 19.41–47	Rom. 8.12–17	Matt. 7.15–21
10 AP 9 AT	1 Cor. 12.2–11	Luke 18.9–14	1 Cor. 10.1–13	Luke 16.1–9
11 AP 10 AT	1 Cor. 15.1–10	Mark 7.31–37	1 Cor. 12.1–11	Luke 19.41–47
12 AP 11 AT	2 Cor. 3.4–9	Luke 10.23–37	1 Cor. 15.1–11	Luke 18.9–14

*** There was an 'extra' Sunday in *MR*, a hangover from the time before Trinity Sunday (instituted 1334) was celebrated, and this anomaly continued until Vatican II's reform of the calendar. BCP's counting the Sundays 'after Trinity' was the logical step once Pentecost was no longer the last date regulated by the fall of Easter; however, *MR* continued the medieval formula 'after Pentecost' until *RL*. It is now *CWL* that has vestiges of the medieval system!

Table A6.1 (continued)

Day	Tridentine Missal		BCP	
	Epistle	Gospel	Epistle	Gospel
13 AP 12 AT	Gal. 3.16–22	Luke 17.11–19	2 Cor. 3.4–9	Mark 7.31–37
14 AP 13 AT	Gal. 5.16–24	Matt. 6.24–33	Gal. 3.16–32	Luke 10.23–37
15 AP 14 AT	Gal. 5.25–26; 6.1–10	Luke 7.11–16	Gal. 5.16–24	Luke 17.11–19
16 AP 15 AT	Eph. 3.13–21	Luke 14.1–11	Gal. 6.11–18	Matt. 6.24–34
17 AP 16 AT	Eph. 4.1–6	Matt. 22.34–46	Eph. 3.13–21	Luke 7.11–17
18 AP 17 AT	1 Cor. 1.4–8	Matt. 9.1–8	Eph. 4.1–6	Luke 14.1–11
19 AP 18 AT	Eph. 4.23–28	Matt. 22.1–14	1 Cor. 1.4–8	Matt. 22.34–46
20 AP 19 AT	Eph. 5.15–21	John 4.46–53	Eph. 4.17–32	Matt. 9.1–8
21 AP 20 AT	Eph. 6.10–17	Matt. 18.23–35	Eph. 5.15–21	Matt. 22.1–14
22 AP 21 AT	Phil. 1.6–11	Matt. 22.15–21	Eph. 6.10–20	John 4.46–54
23 AP 22 AT	Phil. 3.17–21; 4.1–3	Matt. 9.18–26	Phil. 1.3–11	Matt. 18.21–35
23 AT****			Phil. 3.17–21	Matt. 22.15–21
24 AT			Col. 1.3–12	Matt. 9.18–26
Last Sunday	Col. 1.9–14	Matt. 24.15–35	Jer. 23.5–8	John 6.5–14
24 AP 25 AT				

**** MR used a slightly different method for filling the time in those years when Easter fell 'early'; note the rubric in BCP after 25 AT.

Appendix 7

The two systems of numbering the Psalms

Table A7.1 Psalm numbering, Hebrew and Greek

Hebrew text of the Old Testament Used by RCL, CWL, and most Bibles and hymnals printed in English	*Septuagint text of the Old Testament* Used by RL and official Catholic liturgical books
1–8	1–8
9–10	9
11–113	10–112
114–115	113
116	114–115
117–146	116–145
147	146–147
148–150	148–150

Further reading

The first step in gaining a deeper understanding of the Lectionary is to read the 1982 edition of *The General Instruction on the Lectionary*. Although it is intended solely as a guide to *RL*, it gives the best insight into the thinking of those who designed the Lectionary. It can be found in several places on the web; the most convenient is at <www.liturgyoffice.org.uk/Resources/ Rites/Lectionary.pdf>. This can then be set in its own context by looking at Bugnini 1990.

A good, quick introduction to the notion of a lectionary can be found in Allen 2002. If you want to examine the history of the Lectionary, see Palazzo 1998. To study the content of the present liturgy, in terms of its overall structure, the most convenient work is Bonneau 1998. O'Loughlin 2007 and 2010b provide a short and a shorter survey of the Lectionary's content; these two works, like that of Bonneau, are focused on *RL*. For a straightforward survey of *RCL*, Bower 1996 is still extremely convenient. For an overview of the two forms of the Lectionary along with an analysis of how they are used by their different constituencies, see West 1997.

When it comes to resources for working with the Lectionary, there is a profusion of material – and every journal aimed at ministers (and almost every church-based website) contains material. But 'let the reader beware': quite a lot of what is presented as 'resources for the Lectionary' is simply exegesis of excerpts from the Scriptures which pays little heed either to the structure of the Lectionary or to the liturgical setting in which these passages are celebrated.

What follows are the details of the materials to which I have referred in the course of this book, and in which specific topics can be followed up in more depth.

Aageson, James W., 1992, 'Lectionary: Early Jewish Lectionaries' in Freedman, 1992, 4, 270–1.

Achtemeier, P. J., 1990, '*Omne verbum sonat*: The New Testament and the Oral Environment of Late Western Antiquity', *Journal of Biblical Literature* 109, 3–27.

Allen, Horace T., 2002, 'Lectionaries' in Bradshaw 2002, 274–7.

Bauckham, Richard (ed.), 1998, *The Gospels for All Christians: Rethinking Gospel Audiences*, Cambridge and Grand Rapids, MI, Eerdmans.

Bettenson, Henry, 1963, *Documents of the Christian Church*, Oxford, Oxford University Press (first edn 1943).

Bonneau, Normand, 1998, *The Sunday Lectionary: Ritual Word, Paschal Shape*, Collegeville, MN, Liturgical Press.

Bower, Peter C. (ed.), 1996, *Handbook for the Revised Common Lectionary*, Louisville, KY, Westminster John Knox Press.

Bradshaw, Paul F. (ed.), 2001, *A Companion to Common Worship*, vol. 1, London, SPCK.

Bradshaw, Paul F., 2002, *The New SCM Dictionary of Liturgy and Worship*, London, SCM Press.

Bradshaw, Paul F., 2009, *Reconstructing Early Christian Worship*, London, SPCK.

Bradshaw, Paul F., and Maxwell E. Johnson, 2011, *The Origins of Feasts, Fasts and Seasons in Early Christianity*, London, SPCK.

Bugnini, Annibale, 1990, *The Reform of the Liturgy 1948–1975*, Collegeville, MN, Liturgical Press.

Buxton, Richard F., 2002, 'Quinquagesima' in Bradshaw 2002, 397–8.

Chilton, Bruce, 2002, *Redeeming Time: The Wisdom of Ancient Jewish and Christian Festal Calendars*, Peabody, MA, Hendrickson.

Croegaert, A., 1958, *The Mass: A Liturgical Commentary, Vol. 1* (reprinted in 1963 as *The Mass of the Catechumens: A Liturgical Commentary*), London, Burns and Oates.

De Lubac, Henri, 1959, *Medieval Exegesis: The Four Senses of Scripture* (English translation: Edinburgh, T&T Clark, 1998 and 2000).

Fenwick, John, and Bryan Spinks, 1995, *Worship in Transition: The Twentieth Century Liturgical Movement*, Edinburgh, T&T Clark.

Flannery, Austin, 1975, *Vatican Council II: The Conciliar and Post Conciliar Documents*, Wilmington, DE, Scholarly Resources (and many other editions).

Freedman, David Noel (ed.), 1992, *The Anchor Bible Dictionary*, New York, Doubleday.

Giles, Gordon, 2001, 'The Sunday Lectionary' in Bradshaw 2001, 225–35.

Hageman, Howard G., 1982, 'A Brief Study of the English Lectionary', *Worship* 56, 356–64.

Hebblethwaite, David, 2004, *Liturgical Revision in the Church of England 1984–2004: The Working of the Liturgical Commission* (*Joint Liturgical Studies 57*), Cambridge, Grove Books.

Hill, C. E., 2006, 'Papias of Hierapolis', *Expository Times* 117, 309–15.

Illich, Ivan, 1993, *In the Vineyard of the Text: A Commentary to Hugh's Didascalicon*, Chicago, IL and London, University of Chicago Press.

Koester, Helmut, 1989, 'From the Kerygma-Gospel to Written Gospel', *New Testament Studies* 35, 361–81.

Kwok Pui-lan, 2010, 'Spirituality for the Cathedral and Bazaar Mind', *Spiritus: A Journal of Christian Spirituality* 10, 271–5.

Lathrop, Gordon W., 2003, *Holy Ground: A Liturgical Cosmology*, Minneapolis, MN, Augsburg Fortress.

McHugh, John, 1975, *The Mother of Jesus in the New Testament*, London, Darton, Longman and Todd.

McLuhan, Marshall, 1962, *The Gutenberg Galaxy: The Making of Typographic Man*, London, Routledge and Kegan Paul.

Meier, John P., 1994, *A Marginal Jew: Mentor, Message, and Miracles*, New York, Yale University Press.

Mitchell, Leonel L., 1977, *The Meaning of Ritual*, New York, Paulist Press.

Mowinckel, Sigmund, 1962, *The Psalms in Israel's Worship*, Oxford, Blackwell.

O'Loughlin, Thomas, 1998, 'Christ and the Scriptures: The Chasm between Modern and Pre-modern Exegesis', *The Month* 259, 475–85.

O'Loughlin, Thomas, 2000, 'A Woman's Plight and the Western Fathers' in L. J. Kreitzer and D. W. Rooke (eds), *Ciphers in the Sand: Interpretations of the Woman Taken in Adultery (John 7.53—8.11)*, Sheffield, Sheffield Academic Press, 83–104.

O'Loughlin, Thomas, 2004, *Liturgical Resources for Lent and Eastertide: Years A, B, and C*, Dublin, Columba Press.

O'Loughlin, Thomas, 2006, *Liturgical Resources for Advent and Christmastide: Years A, B, and C*, Dublin, Columba Press.

O'Loughlin, Thomas, 2007, *Explaining the Lectionary for Readers*, Dublin, Columba Press.

O'Loughlin, Thomas, 2007a, '"Would you Read?": The Task of the Lector', *Anaphora* 1.2, 19–36.

O'Loughlin, Thomas, 2009, 'Liturgical Evolution and the Fallacy of the Continuing Consequence', *Worship* 83, 312–23.

O'Loughlin, Thomas, 2009a, 'Losing Mystery in History: The Challenge of Recalling the Nativity' in J. Corley (ed.), *New Perspectives on the Nativity*, London, T&T Clark International, 180–99.

O'Loughlin, Thomas, 2010, *The Didache: A Window on the Earliest Christians*, London, SPCK and Grand Rapids, MI, Baker Academic.

O'Loughlin, Thomas, 2010a, 'Eucharistic Celebrations: the Chasm between Idea and Reality', *New Blackfriars* 91, 423–38.

O'Loughlin, Thomas, 2010b, *Sunday Mass Readings: The Thinking behind the Lectionary*, London, Catholic Truth Society.

O'Loughlin, Thomas, 2011, 'The Missionary Strategy of the *Didache*', *Transformation* 28, 77–92.

Palazzo, Eric, 1998, *A History of Liturgical Books from the Beginning to the Thirteenth Century*, Collegeville, MN, Liturgical Press.

Parker, D. C., 2008, *An Introduction to the New Testament Manuscripts and Their Texts*, Cambridge, Cambridge University Press.

Parvis, Paul, 2008, 'Justin Martyr', *Expository Times* 120, 53–61.

Ramshaw, Gail, 1988, *Worship: Searching for Language*, Washington, DC, Pastoral Press.

Ramshaw, Gail, 1990, 'The First Testament in Christian Lectionaries', *Worship* 64, 494–510.

Rothenbuhler, Eric W., 1998, *Ritual Communication: From Everyday Conversation to Mediated Ceremony*, London, Sage.

Schwartz, Barry, 1982, 'The Social Context of Commemoration: A Study in Collective Memory', *Social Forces* 61, 374–402.

Seasoltz, Kevin, 1966, *The New Liturgy: A Documentation 1903–1965*, New York, Herder and Herder.

Seasoltz, Kevin, 1980, *New Liturgy, New Laws*, Collegeville, MN, Liturgical Press.

Sherwin-White, A. N., 1969, *Fifty Letters of Pliny*, Oxford, Oxford University Press.

Sloyan, Gerard S., 1987, 'Is Church Teaching Neglected when the Lectionary is Preached?' *Worship* 61, 126–40.

Sloyan, Gerard S., 1989, 'Some Suggestions for a Biblical Three-Year Lectionary', *Worship* 63, 521–35.

Smith, Dennis E., 1991, 'The Messianic Banquet Reconsidered' in B. A. Pearson (ed.), *The Future of Early Christianity: Essays in Honor of Helmut Koester*, Minneapolis, MN, Fortress, 64–73.

Smith, Jonathan Z., 2001, 'A Twice-Told Tale: The History of the History of Religion's History', *Numen* 48, 134–46.

Spinks, Bryan D., 2010, *The Worship Mall: Contemporary Responses to Contemporary Culture*, London, SPCK.

Stanton, Graham N., 2004, *Jesus and Gospel*, Cambridge, Cambridge University Press.

Taussig, Hal, 2009, *In the Beginning Was the Meal: Social Experimentation and Early Christian Identity*, Minneapolis, MN, Augsburg Fortress.

Thompson, Michael B., 1998, 'The Holy Internet: Communication between Churches in the First Christian Generation' in Bauckham 1998, 49–70.

West, Fritz, 1997, *Scripture and Memory: The Ecumenical Hermeneutic of the Three-Year Lectionary*, Collegeville, MN, Liturgical Press.

Index of biblical references

References given in tables of readings are omitted.

Index of names and subjects

References to days and seasons within the liturgical year mentioned in tables are omitted.

ND - #0051 - 270325 - C0 - 216/138/12 - PB - 9780281065875 - Gloss Lamination